COMMUNITY
A Critical Response

KEY CONCEPTS
IN THE SOCIAL SCIENCES

GENERAL EDITORS

PHILIP RIEFF
Benjamin Franklin Professor of Sociology
University of Pennsylvania

BRYAN R. WILSON
Reader in Sociology, University of Oxford
Fellow of All Souls College

Key Concepts in the Social Sciences

COMMUNITY
A Critical Response

Joseph R. Gusfield

Harper & Row Publishers
New York, Evanston, San Francisco

First ENGLISH LANGUAGE edition published 1975

LIBRARY OF CONGRESS CATALOG
CARD NUMBER: 75-5389

STANDARD BOOK NUMBER: 0-06-136176-3

Sue Miller, Jessica Diaz,
Nancy Jimenez-Vera, Beverly Strong
Thanks

PREFACE

Intellectual products reflect many parts of a life. Two experiences seem of special significance for me in writing this volume. One stems from residence and research in India as a Fulbright Lecturer in the early 1960s. Subsequent research and writing on social change and development theory owed a great deal to that experience, as does this current effort. Some aspects of this book were first developed while I was an Associate Member of the University of Illinois Center for Advanced Studies, in 1965. I am indebted to many friends and former colleagues at Patna University and at the Delhi School of Economics from whom I learned what little I know of India.

The second intellectual experience has been more recent. It comes from exposure to recent trends in phenomenological sociology. For this I am in debt to my colleagues and graduate students in the Department of Sociology at the University of California, San Diego. The discussions of the past seven years have been a feast of much satisfaction.

I am deeply grateful to Philip Rieff for a critical reading of an early draft and for valued suggestions. The final revision was completed while I was a Guggenheim Foundation Fellow and a visiting Scholar at the London School of Economics. This expresses my keen appreciation to the Guggenheim Foundation for their support and to the London School of Economics for kindly making their facilities avail-

able to me. The dedication page expresses my gratitude to an
office staff that has been invaluable to me on many occasions
and projects, including this one.

   As always, writing is a journey which leaves the traveller
changed and wishing that he might undo his path and re-
trace his tour somewhat differently.

La Jolla, California
July, 1975

CONTENTS

3
COMMUNITY IN SOCIETY:
CONCEPTS AS SYSTEMS   53

4
THE SEARCH FOR COMMUNITY:
CONCEPTS AS UTOPIAS   83

INTRODUCTION

Words that sociologists use often look familiar but are not. Concepts like "role," "culture," "authority," and "mobility" are words in common usage. In the vocabulary of the sociologist they take on particular meanings that differ from their usage outside of the sociological context. The same is true in other disciplines. The "money" of the economist is not the layman's money nor is the physicist's "energy" or "mass" what the student has understood by these terms in his everyday life. You must be prepared to adopt a more deliberate attentiveness toward the concepts of sociology if you wish to find your way through the thickets of language that surround sociological insights and understandings.

The concept "community" is among those words which the student already has in his or her repertoire of thought even before he learns the word "sociology." "Community welfare," "community work," "community fund" represent one kind of use. "The community of scholars," "the Italian-American community," "the community of Atlanta" suggests still another use. You have heard talk about "creating a sense of community," "the lack of community" and "community feeling." The first of these, as in "community welfare," seems to refer to an all-inclusive, public interest as contrasted to special or partial interests. The second, as in "community of scholars," appears to talk about a special closeness or bond which unites some persons and differentiates them from others. The bond may be one of life styles, or ethnic origin or territory. The third usage, as in "the lack of community" seems to point to a particular kind of human relationship rather than a special kind of group.

All of this is probably confusing to the student. Which way is the sociologist using the word, or is he or she using it in some quite novel sense? If you browse in the library or the bookshop, you will find books with titles like *The Quest for Community, Commitment and Community, Community Power Structure, The Community, The American Community, Community Studies.* At this point you may be tempted to drop all of them and run to your class in vertebrate anatomy where at least you can match words to tangible objects, to things you can touch and feel and see. The tibia and the ulna will not differ from one anatomist to another, but "community" is not so static a concept.

How shall I talk about how sociologists talk? My dilemma can be thought of as a choice between clarity and utility. It would be simpler if I could define the concept and point, unambiguously, to what it conveys. This would represent a consistent and uniform meaning, about which consensus exists among sociologists. But it would result in distortion and inaccuracy. It would not help the student to read his or her way through a library of books in order to grasp the different usages and the contexts and reasons for those diversities. Neither would it help the student to cope with the phenomena of ambiguity and conflict which characterize sociology.

In a very influential book—*The Structure of Scientific Revolutions*—the historian and philosopher of science, Thomas Kuhn, has concluded that at any given time, scientists operate within a set of general principles, ideas and problems about which they are agreed. This consensus makes it possible to perform scientific operations in a routine and predictable fashion, which he calls "normal science." Epochal changes occur when these fundamental sources of agreement undergo criticism, revision and replacement and normal science itself becomes a matter of debate. It is the normality of science at any specific period which makes it possible to codify and state the major concepts, principles and methods in the form of textbooks and recipes for "doing science."

Kuhn's insights, however, are not readily transported into the social, or human, sciences. Consensus is seldom the mark of social science and normality at best an aspiration rather than a reality. Textbooks, of course, are written but they are notoriously poor maps to disputed territory. I hope that this work will help the student appreciate why this situation is characteristic of the human sciences.

Because concepts in the social sciences are part of human assessments and concerns, they are utilized in contexts of doubt, conflict and hope. They are used as means to select out of the confusion and multiplicity of events the character- istics and elements which are related to the purposes and interests of their users. We cannot assume that there is a direct and clear relation between the concept and some reference point in the real world. This feature of human selectivity and human concerns makes for differences in the meanings of concepts.

It is this shifting and differing quality of sociological con- cepts that makes it necessary to understand them as aspects of a context and a history. This is what I am trying to do with the word "community" in this essay: to explore and examine its use in sociological contexts, in the light of its historical development.

Before plunging into the heated pool of critical analysis, however, it will be useful to make some introductory remarks about "community" which will prepare the student for the analysis to follow. As I emphasize in the body of this study, sociological concepts must be understood in their context of contrasts, by what they point away from as well as what they point toward.

Two major usages of "community" should be distinguished at the outset. In the first, the territorial, the concept appears in a context of location, physical territory, geographical con- tinuity. This is its meaning, in part, in studies of such

B

phenomena as "community power structure," "the urban community," and "community studies." Such studies concentrate on locality as distinguished from more remote physical relationships. The town, the village, the neighborhood, the city—these are the loci of such community studies. The thrust of work in this area of study is to understand what is occurring to such community entities. What is the structure of authority, of class relationships, of political governance within that area? How are these entities changing?

The second usage, the relational, points to the quality or character of human relationships, without reference to location. Here, studies are oriented toward the ways in which group members cooperate and conflict—to the existence or absence of bonds of similarity and sympathy, to what unites or differentiates a collectivity of people. In this usage, community is a characteristic of some human relationships rather than a bounded and defined group, as it is in the first, or territorial, usage.

The two uses of community are not sharply exclusive. The major problem of much of the study of the community as territory has been the examination of how small and large communities, urban and rural communities, neighborhoods and suburbs achieve or diminish communal relationships. As I will indicate in later chapters, this area of interest has grown out of the context of community in the second usage, the relational. It has done so because a great concern of studies of community as a relationship has been with the impact of the social changes toward larger and more diverse social units. The distinction between "community" and "society" is thus a fundamental focus of this essay, and is treated in detail.

I have chosen to place my emphasis in this work on the second usage of community—as relational. I have done so because it seems to me that this use has had the strongest impact on many areas of sociological study and social thought. It has been of special significance for the analysis of social change in both Western societies and the new nations of Asia and Africa. It has been important to the development

of theories and hypotheses in a variety of branches of sociology.

Let me close this introduction with a last word of caution.
Concepts in sociology are often used in ways which are
normative as well as descriptive. By this, I mean that concepts help us to determine the significance of events and
processes as well as merely describing them. They develop
in connection with problems of morals, politics, ethics and
human choice and enable us to pick out and assess those
activities which have relevance for our interests, purposes
and sentiments.

For this reason, concepts are best understood by seeing
how they are used, by examining their historical developments, by showing their contrasting concepts and even by
criticizing their claims and uses. That is why I have not
offered the student a definition of "community." To do so
might make my task simpler, but it would distort the work of
the sociologist and limit the value of this study to the student.

1

COMMUNITY AND SOCIETY
Concepts as Ideologies

Introduction: Concepts and Counter-concepts

In the parade of ideas, concepts seldom march alone. We understand and identify both by pointing and by distinguishing. We show what is by showing what it is not. Concepts and counter-concepts exist in a necessary symbiosis, each revealing the meaning of the other. Polarisms, dualities and oppositional terms are abundant in the social sciences. The corpus of sociological work is filled with these and other typologies: caste and class; rural and urban; primary and secondary, traditional and rational authority; culture and social organization.

The concept of "community" must also be understood as one side of a pervasive, influential and significant contrast. The dichotomy of "community and society" has been the major framework within the poles of which sociologists have set their discussions of human associations and social changes. These two concepts have been central terms in the discussions, the research, the theories and the understandings in which social scientists have tried to understand the present, compare it with the past and imagine and affect the future.

In the talk about human behavior, concepts connote as well as denote. They carry an emotional freight which holds vivid preferences and values as well as descriptions in neutral colors. "Community and society" has served as the arena within which sociologists, historians and other social scientists have struggled to assess as well as to understand the direction of the modern world. The opposition in terms has carried along with it a running dialogue both political and philosophical in its origins and significance.

Within this study of community and society, I will emphasize both aspects of the concepts: their use as devices to describe and analyze human associations, and their usage in the continuing intellectual evaluation of the present and its direction and significance. Of necessity, one aspect cannot be discussed in the complete absence of the other. However, in Chapters 1 and 4, I will be most concerned with the concepts as they impinge on the debate over the quality and worth of modern culture. In Chapters 2 and 3, I will shift emphases and focus upon the scientific character of the concepts, their use in description and analysis.

There are then two dimensions of analysis between which I shall travel in this essay. One is the *scientific*. Here, we assess concepts for their utility in enabling us to understand, clarify and predict human actions. But it is part of the assertion of this work that these two central concepts in sociology have also acted as *metaphorical images* of virtuous or vicious human associations—depictions of ideals and evils to be sought or to be avoided. Analyzed in this fashion, they cannot be discussed solely as scientific, utilitarian concepts. Within this dimension, they must be seen as mythic images and as aspects of ideologies and utopian doctrines.

This outline of the discussion of community and society constitutes the major theme or plot of this essay. But there is an underlying and explicit subsidiary plot which is methodological, while the major plot is substantive. Here I am concerned with the method of elaborating oppositional types as itself a process to be discussed and assessed. My assertion is critical. Woven throughout the four chapters is the theme of the dichotomy of community and society as abused and distorting devices for scientific understanding of social change and human association.

This plot too, has its double dimensions. The critique of

the scientific utility of the community-society dualism also carries its metaphorical usage. It too becomes a way of stating an alternate ideology, another utopia. Taken together, these two themes—the exposition of the concepts and the critique of their usage—constitute an analysis of the relation between science and metaphor, between fact and value in the social sciences. As my argument unfolds, I hope to display the ways in which each supports and upholds the other.

Nostalgia and Disgust: Twin Views of Community

In the Western world of ideas, the nineteenth century was an era acutely aware of the future. The American and the French revolutions had opened the curtain on the 1800s with a new doctrine of citizenship, equality and individual rights. The Industrial Revolution was creating a new order of human institutions and classes. Populations had grown. Nationalism appeared as a principle of solidarity and new nations emerged to change the political map of Europe. It was an era of quarrel and protest; of workers' discontent and citizens' revolt. Self-consciously the men and women of the nineteenth century were aware that what had been the outlines of human associations for many centuries was now old; that a new world of human relationships and human culture was coming into being. It is this perceived and profound change in history that occupied the attention of thinkers of the period.

The theorists whose writings gave rise to much of contemporary sociology lived and wrote during the last half of the nineteenth and early part of the twentieth centuries. They were acutely sensitive to living in the ruins of an old social order amid the envisioned outlines of a new one beyond the horizon. Although the old revolutions were over, their significance and their continuing direction were still matters of fervent dispute. The virtues and vices of the traditional and the modern were debated, analyzed, defended and attacked.

In such a period, a widespread interest in the direction of history is understandable. Writing in different European countries, often with distinctive intellectual cultures and sometimes unaware of each other's works, the forerunners and progenitors of contemporary sociology produced a set of writings which, while distinct in many ways, yet contained the underlying agreement that European social life was changing in a common direction. Karl Marx, writing in *The Communist Manifesto* (1848) saw that the world of feudalism had given way to the market commodity society of industrial capitalism. Sir Henry Maine, in *Ancient Law*, and later in *Village Communities of the East and West* (1871), visualized the transition as one from a form of tradition-bound *status* to one of individualistic *contract*. In his *law of three stages*, Auguste Comte (1830–92) depicted mankind as having passed through the religious and the metaphysical stages and now on the brink of the final, positive (scientific) stage. In several works, Herbert Spencer (1857) set forth his law of social evolution: society was moving from a homogeneous structure to one of heterogeneous structure in which exchange was the keynote of human relationships. Émile Durkheim (1887) expressed the transition as one from mechanical to organic solidarity. Writing in the early twentieth century, Max Weber used the concepts of traditional authority and legal-rational authority to express the great changes he saw in the modern period. It was the German sociologist, Ferdinand Tönnies, who gave later generations the most widely-used terms to define and discuss the common perspective of these thinkers. The title of his book (*Gemeinschaft und Gesellschaft*) has remained the major concept of present-day sociologists for different human associations: *Gemeinschaft* (Community) and *Gesellschaft* (Society).

What all of these writers had in common in their schemes of social change was the view of their era as being the culmination of a major stage in the evolution of human associations. "The present", wrote Comte, "is big with the future." A common belief in *social evolution* underlay their various theories. They saw the social changes of their time as moving the world along a line of direction away from one point and toward another. The directionality of these changes was inevitable and not reversible. In this area of their writings, the early sociologists were neither believers in cycle theories of change nor in the unpredictability and diffuseness of major trends in history.[1*]

A second common idea united these thinkers. They believed that the changes of the industrial and democratic revolutions meant the rapid disappearance of one kind of human association and its replacement by another. They saw two types of human associations, each constituting a systematic arrangement of consistent parts and each contradicting the other. The forms of the modern broke sharply with the dominant features of pre-nineteenth-century life. The present was a more individuated and individualistic social organization than the past; one in which bonds of group loyalties and emotional attachments gave way to the rationalistic ties of utilitarian interests and uniform law. It was a world in which the ordered and accepted structure of privileges and duties between unequals was blown away in the winds of class struggle and equality of person; in which the common beliefs of religion were battered by the attacks of secular and scientific argument.

Nostalgia for the old and disgust for the new were evident among some sociologists and philosophers. For these, the loss of community was the lamentable fact of their period in history. As Nisbet has written of Comte, "the ghost of traditional community hovers over his sociology."[2] For the traditionalists, the new world of economic logic, political interest groups, mass electorates and exchange-based market relationships could only mean the destruction of a stable environment and an authority essential to human well-being. They mourned the impending decline of the small and static local areas of neighborhood, kinship and parish. They saw chaos in the disappearance of a system of ordered and respectful relations between stable classes. They would have

---

* Notes are to be found at the end of each chapter.

agreed with Oliver Goldsmith's earlier depiction of the results of social change in his poem *The Deserted Village*:

> Ill fares the land
>
> To hastening ills a prey,
> Where wealth accumulates
>
> And men decay.

The loss lamented by one group was loudly cheered by another. Writers as diverse in their politics as Marx and Spencer saw the traditional world of the past as coercive, limiting and demoralizing. The destruction of the old world of communal patterns could only be a source of satisfaction. As an heir to the enlightenment belief in progress through science, Marx saw much value in a capitalism that had destroyed "the idiocy of rural life." For the modernists, the new rational character of modern life meant the end of those constraints on human equality and economic affluence from which mankind had suffered for much of the human past. They saw contractual relations bringing about an end to the tyranny of custom, and they pronounced the individualism of the new order as a positive virtue. The bondage of material scarcity and disease and the coercion of custom and ignorance would disappear. It was not only Marx and Engels who believed that the new man of the future would make the leap to the "Kingdom of Freedom."

The debate about the direction of history which absorbed these early sociologists has continued and has given to contemporary thought one of its dominant themes. A litany of loss permeates one broad segment of sociology and provides a center about which cluster voices of assent and criticism. Within this circle of dialogue men and women utilize the concepts of community and society as ways of marking their place in the disputes.

*Émile Durkheim: The Sources and Significance of
Community in Modern Life*

Émile Durkheim's seminal work, *The Division of Labor in
Society* (1893) will be the starting-point for an exploration of
the "community-society" dichotomy. It illustrates the
development of this dualism as an aspect of sociological
analysis and provides us with a deeper probe into the sociological debate about modern life. Durkheim's work and his
life reflected many facets of the intellectual and political
responses of late nineteenth and early twentieth-century
Europe to the issues of cultural and social change. This great
French scholar has remained a vital influence on contemporary sociology. *The Division of Labor* represents a major work
of both theory and research in the study of social change. In
it Durkheim continued the social evolutionary motif of
Comte and of Spencer, but he also provided a critique of
both.

It is useful to read a work in the social sciences through
discovering its polemical nexus. This is the argument, thesis
or theory which the author has come to disown, attack and
criticize. In *The Division of Labor* there are two such
nexuses. Against the assertions of Comte and the French
traditionalists, Durkheim presents the liberal or modernist
view; one which upholds the values of the modern society.
Against Spencer and those who viewed modern society as
held together solely by bonds of utility and exchange,
Durkheim saw the modern forms of human association producing their own type of social bond.

In Durkheim's evolutionary scheme, the transition from
small, provincial, homogeneous settlements to the contemporary large urban centers was accompanied by a shift
in the characteristic social bond by which human cooperation and predictability is possible. He described this shift as
one from *mechanical solidarity* to *organic solidarity*. The
first, mechanical solidarity, was the result of the similarity of
traditions, beliefs, and activities that characterized the small,

agricultural villages. It was mechanical as compared to the organic, in that people were comparatively similar in skills, ideas and functions. In the modern cities and the new societies coming into being such similarities are diminished. Men perform highly divergent and specialized tasks. With the aggregation of dense populations and dispersed social areas, the similarity of custom and belief is weakened.

Unlike Comte and the French conservatives, Durkheim did not find the disappearance of mechanical solidarity lamentable. It did not signify the disappearance of social bonds and the emergence of social anarchy because the new social form generated its own and different social bond: it was a new form of human association. An *organic solidarity* develops, based on the differences between men rather than upon their similarities. In a human association where people pursue highly specialized and developed skills and functions, they complement each other, depend on each other and develop social codes of duty toward each other. Where others found social destruction in the development of industry, cities and specialization, Durkheim saw in them new forms of social organization.

> In the first, what we call society is a more or less organized totality of beliefs and sentiments; common to all members of the group; this is the collective type. On the other hand, the society in which we are solidary in the second instance is a system of special functions which definite relations unite.[3]

It would be a mistake to interpret Durkheim as an exponent of the utilitarian or economic man as the source of social cohesion in the modern world. In the concept of economic exchange, Herbert Spencer had provided a source for modern social solidarity based on rational self-interest. Critics might say that he had "reduced" social life to cold calculation and destroyed the non-rational faith essential to social order. Durkheim was specific in his criticism of Spencerian sociology. Contracts and exchange presupposed a structure of trust and belief in the morality of promises and reciprocal relations; in the authority of legal and political institutions. Men's occupational attachments and their personal development around goals of specialized achievement provided a distinctively modern morality; individualistic in the sense of stressing the unique and the specialized yet social in being regulated by a moral code.

At the time that he first published *The Division of Labor*, Durkheim thus presented a two-sided "answer" to the problem of the modern era. Toward those looking back to the past with longing and to the future with foreboding, he provided a contrasting vision of a social life quite capable of organization and viability. Toward those who saw only economic utilities as a source of human mutuality, he pointed out the normative and institutional premises of the economic market and showed that these were possible in urban, modern life. Toward those for whom the individualistic credo of the new society was a sign of anarchy, Durkheim displayed a view of individualism as itself a moral order and consistent with social cohesion. The nineteenth century's prognosis of the decline of community, of mechanical solidarity, by no means need to be read, in Durkheim's work, as the elimination of ethical or moral human arrangements and their replacement by self-interested, utility-motivated individuals. Society had its own distinctive order. It too was moral in its source and in its significance.

Sociological Types: Community and Society

As a system of analysis and a theory of social change, Durkheim's distinction between two forms of social organization shared much of the social evolutionary schemes of his era. It posed one type of human association as a contrast to another and it described the general direction of historical change as the decline of one type and the ascendency of another.

Durkheim's distinction between "mechanical" and

"organic" solidarity has been echoed in many forms. The specific construction of "community and society" derives from frequent English translations of the typology of Gemeinschaft and Gesellschaft, enunciated by Ferdinand Tönnies in his work of the same title, published in 1887. Tönnies placed more emphasis than did Durkheim on the difference between deliberately formed associations for rational achievement of mutual goals (society) and those naturally developed forms of organizations which have intrinsic and non-logical values to them (community). For sociologists, as for other theorists mentioned, such human organizations as kinship, friendship, neighborhood and "folk" are communal; corporations, economic contracts, labor unions and political parties are societal.

The community-society typology might also be seen as distinguishing relationships based on *sentiments*—emotional and intrinsic attachments—from those of *interests*—mutually held goals which prescribe cooperation in their pursuit. The parent-child attachment is illustrative of the communal relationship derived from *sentiment*; the customer-merchant relationship, the example of *interests*. The building blocks of community are thus familial, kin, territorial, ethnic, religious; the sense of being part of a common group where loyalties and obligations rest on affective, emotional elements. Society is made up of groups such as hospitals, schools, courts and organizations where expediency, exchange, mutual interest and rational calculation of gain are the criteria of participation and success.

Max Weber provides us with a formal statement of the distinction between community and society. Using Tönnies' concepts of Gemeinschaft and Gesellschaft, Weber wrote:

A social relationship will be called "communal" (Vergemeinschaftung) if and so far as the orientation of social action—whether in the individual case, on the average, or in the pure type, is based on a subjective feeling of the parties, whether affectual or traditional, that they belong together. A social relationship will be called "associative" (Vergesellschaftung) if and in so far as the orientation of social action within it rests on a rationally motivated adjustment of interests or a similarly motivated agreement, whether the basis of rational judgment be absolute values or reasons of expediency.[4]

"Community" and "society" are used by sociologists to describe two major types of human associations. The use of types and typologies (systems of types) is a characteristic mode of analysis in the social sciences. It gives rise, however, to a number of perplexing questions which create considerable ambiguity in the use of contrasted concepts such as "community and society." These were to cause difficulty for Durkheim in later work, as we shall see. They have also been at the root of misunderstanding and fallacy in theories of social change. Before we can continue the analysis of these concepts we must take an interlude to discuss the issues surrounding the use of typology in social science.

Digression: The Problem of Types in Sociological Analysis

"Community" and "society" do not describe any known, actually existing society nor any of historical existence. They are *analytical* and not *empirical* terms; concepts invented to help the analyst think about and talk about change and human associations. As such, they are products of human imagination and not descriptions of a real world. No permanent human association can be found which contains all the attributes of community and none of society; in which there is no division of labor, all actions are void of rational interest and all cooperative activity is regulated by bonds of sentiment. Contrariwise, society is never found in any pure form. Even in seemingly economic organizations, such as factories, there are loyalties, sentiments and emotional ties which emerge among workers and between the echelons of authority. These limit and distort the application of economic rationality. People are acting out of a sense of community.

Even between parent and child, elements of economic arrangements can and often do play an important role. People act societally.

The concrete and the empirical, the actual, existent reality, is too diffuse, fluctuating and ambiguous to be grasped and talked about in ways which yield understanding, direction and significance. Types provide the analyst with a way of talking and thinking about events, processes and experiences to yield a more usable knowledge, to develop hypotheses, to deduce consequences and to make predictions. We can think about what would be true insofar as particular associations are communal or societal. We can describe specific associations as more or less communal or societal. But at the same time, types are not themselves the same as empirical, descriptive events. Human realities seldom emerge in such stark and pure forms. "... theoretical models (whether treated as real or fictitious) are not literally constructed; the heart of the method consists in talking in a certain way."[5]

The dilemma is a crucial one for sociological method. On the one hand, the complex, fluid character of situations and events can only be described accurately as particular and nonrepeatable. On the other hand, situations and events are experienced through a screen of general types and the sociologist must utilize typologies if he is to achieve general knowledge.

A frequently used device to solve this dilemma has been Max Weber's invention of the "ideal-type." This is an imagined construction, a

> ... conceptual pattern [which] brings together certain relationships and events of historical life into a complex, which is conceived as an internally consistent system... It is not a description of reality but it aims to give unambiguous means of expression to such a description.[6]

Examples of ideal-types are such frequently used concepts as "bureaucracy," "capitalism," "modern society" and "community." Weber was quite specific in indicating that such types are *not* averages or descriptions, but are heuristic tools, helpful in understanding reality but in themselves not a version of the real situations.

One of the great dangers in the use of ideal-types is *reification*—treating an abstract, analytical term as if it were descriptive and empirical. Having typed the contemporary social situation as "modern society" the individual events and situations are then seen as ordered and organized into a consistent system containing the components of "modern" and the coherence of a "society." In this process the type [an idea] has been transformed into a thing. (The Latin for "thing" is *res*, the root of reification.)

In using type as paired opposites, the sociologist heightens the understanding of each. He also provides a set of poles between which concrete instances can be ranged; more or less of one type or another. In talking about change specific cases and periods can be described as moving toward one or another pole. There is a danger in this process, however. Empirical events and situations may be classified and treated *as if* they can be described by only one of the pair of opposing types. Coexistence is implicitly denied.

In current sociological usage, the concepts of "community and society" have emerged as opposites in an almost zero-sum form. That is, whatever accentuates society diminishes community, and vice versa. The sum is zero. Reality is made out to be one *or* the other; communal *or* societal. This minimizes the ambivalence and ambiguity in much concrete social action. The vice of such pure typologies is that they hide the crucial impurity of existence and lead the user to minimize the issues of choice which actual existence so often serves.

The paired concepts of sociological theory, then must always be considered *together* when one is engaged in developing testable hypotheses because both concepts are necessary to an analysis of those universal tendencies of social action which, while pointing in opposite directions, are at the same time inextricably linked.[7]

C

A second problem resident in the use of ideal-types lies in the ways in which concepts also embody theories. The evolutionary theories of social change as a transformation of life from community to society are of this nature. If community and society are stated as opposites, their coexistence is transitory and life must move toward one or other pole of the continuum. In using a paired contrast like "feudalism and capitalism" the theory of change is implicit. Each concept of the pair puts together analytical aspects which are seen as unrelated or in conflict with the other. Thus the personal fealty between the dominant noble and the subordinate serf is in conflict with the principle of the free labor contract which is part of the ideal-type "capitalism." By this process a theory of change has been generated in which the system of feudalism will be weakened by free labor contracts and capitalism destroys personal fealty. Situations embodying a coherence of both types are implicitly transitory or temporary.

This ambiguity in the use of sociological types is at the center of the analysis of the community concept and its juxtaposition with the contrast of society. That the various typologies expressing the community-society dualism have carried implicit and explicit ideological commitments alongside their analytical components is understandable when we recognize that such types are constructed by the analysts, not given by empirical situations. They become ways of representing and thinking about the world from some standpoint, from the perspective of some problem which enables the analyst to heighten those aspects of the world which are relevant to his concerns and interests. This becomes apparent when exploring Durkheim's later thought and the current theories of change influenced by the social evolutionary premise of the community-society contrast.

Émile Durkheim: The Reappraisal of Community

Durkheim's own work reveals the difficulties that lie in a rigid use of the "community-society" dualism as a typology of paired contrasts. By 1897, when he published *Suicide*, Durkheim had moved away from the "progressive" view of *Division of Labor in Society*. He still maintained the same distinction between types of societies he had used in the earlier study and related it to types of suicides. Altruistic suicide, exemplified by the military, reflected mechanical solidarity in responding to the norms prescribed by a shared code of honor. Modern societies were more likely to display egoistic or anomic suicide. The sources of egoistic suicide lay in the intensive and compelling aspirations toward achievement dictated by a social code of individualism. The sources of anomic suicide were found in a failure of the society to develop a code of desires which set limits to expectations and desires. The positive relation of depression and prosperity alike to high suicide rates is Durkheim's example of this process. In both forms of suicide the integration of the individual into a socially cohesive group was seen to be essential to well-being. Durkheim therefore now seemed to say that organic solidarity could not be sustained without great risk to the individual personality. Thus he readmitted part of the conservative critique of the individualism of the developing industrial society. Moreover, he found himself unable to depict modern society as a stable society based largely on organic solidarity and the division of labor, even though lacking the integrative elements of earlier societies.

The change in Durkheim's views and the issues raised become clearer when we examine his suggestions for reform. In *Suicide*, he finds the sources of the weak cohesion of many social groups in "the whole of our historical development." "The latter's chief characteristic is to have swept *cleanly* [italics mine—J.G.] away all the older forms of social organization."[8] Durkheim's response is in keeping both with his early view of the "new society" as providing identities based on occupational specialty and with his new appraisal of the loss of communal cohesion. Both in *Suicide* and in the famous preface to the second edition of *The Division of Labor* (edition of 1902), he advocated the development of occupations into communal forms.

He suggested that in the specialized role of occupation might be found another source for cohesion:

> Quite a different group may, then, have the same effect, if it has the same cohesion. Besides the society of faith, of family and of politics, there is one other . . .; that of all workers of the same sort, in association, all who cooperate in the same function, that is the occupational group or corporation.
>
> Identity of origin, culture and occupation makes occupational activity the richest sort of material for a common life.[9]

What is significant here is that Durkheim describes occupation as capable of functioning like religion or family or national sentiment because it provides for a *common* culture. He seems to be saying that the social *malaise* of which suicide is an example is endemic in the social organization of organic solidarity and that only the development of new communal forms in groups, or sub-cultures smaller than the total society can provide the adequate social cohesion needed to produce a "healthier" environment.

Thus Durkheim had come far from the buoyant affirmation of the modern which he had expressed in *The Division of Labor*. He was still, however, not the pessimist who foretold doom and despair in the social change toward the Modern. He was capable of an optimistic prescription that entailed the mix of both communal *and* societal forms, both mechanical and organic solidarity, in the same social organization. This formulation and prediction, however, weakened the utility of his evolutionary scheme and his ideological position in the debate over modernity.

There are two areas of interest in which the community-society distinction has been especially utilized in contemporary sociology. One is the problem of social change in new nations and economically developing countries. The other is a more direct continuation of the problem of modernity in the West, where again the assessment and direction of the Western world is at issue.

The focus of tradition and the modern in recent newly developing nations has made considerable use of these concepts in attempts to understand and discuss contemporary change. One of the earliest and most influential of these schemes was that of the anthropologist, Robert Redfield. He described a contrast between ideal-type "folk" communities and "urban" societies. In his study of four settlements in Yucatan, city, town, peasant village and tribal village (The Folk Culture of Yucatan, 1941), Redfield found an increasing order of cultural disorganization, secularization, and individualization as he went from tribe to city. The urban civilization possessed a more complex division of labor, professional specialization, greater dependence on impersonal institutions, a more developed money economy, greater heterogeneity and less dependence on kinship and on religion than was true of the town, the peasant village and the tribe in descending order. These distinctions between the large, dense and heterogeneous urban society and the small, isolated and homogeneous "folk society" was later (1947) elaborated into the general types of "folk" and "urban" societies, so similar to Durkheim's early formulations. (In later work, Redfield was concerned with peasant communities as intermediate between folk and urban and a distinctive third form of social organization, peasant society.)

As a general scheme for depicting social change and for classifying societies, various forms of the community-society or the folk-urban scheme were also utilized in discussing social and cultural change in the West. Some emphasized the rural and the urban as existing contrasts. Others saw the shift from a religious to a scientific-rational view of the world, from sacred to secular, as the most significant aspect of social change.

Theories of social change were elaborated and revised following World War II, in the context of the independence movements emerging in many new nations and the decline of colonialism. While the earlier theories so frequently emphasized what was lost in the transformation from the world of tradition to the modern, the post-War World II theories occurred in a different climate of concern. Now the problem was how new nations could overcome poverty and political instability to achieve economic growth and political peace. Armed with the evolutionary perspective already present in sociological theory, the words themselves are redolent of evolution. "Development" implies both movement from one stage toward another and the progressive character of that change. "Modernization" implies that the process is necessarily opposite to the pre-existing world of tradition.

The theories of modernization put these concepts into a framework specifying the cultural and/or institutional changes necessary for developing countries to achieve economic development. The expansion of "modern" institutions, such as the economic exchange market, centralized national government, political participation and occupational change and mobility are seen to be impeded by the maintenance of older, "traditional" relationships based on considerations of kinship, caste, religion. Thus particularistic demands of social solidarity to family, lineage or ethnic group are seen in conflict with the needs for economic and political "rationality" for criteria in allocation of resources and decision-making authority. The following states the viewpoint considered here:

It follows directly from the concept of modernization as a process of contention between modernizing and retarding elements ... that the societies we call underdeveloped stand at various stages along the way from traditional to modern status.[10]

It is noticeable that this is again the community-society

contrast but now emerged under different ideological auspices. Where nineteenth-century theorists bemoaned the passage of the past, the modernization theorist finds the disappearance of tradition a welcome and sought-after transformation. It is even prescribed as a means to progress. The linear evolutionary scheme suggests that social change both *requires* and *is developing* conflict between forms of social solidarity which stress unique obligations between members of communal groups and those which emphasize societal interests and mutual goals. Tribal relations, kinship ties, and caste loyalties must, and will, diminish and disappear in the processes of achieving economic progress and development. The communal social system must retreat and give way before the onslaught of the modern if modernity is to be realized.

In its present use, the concept of "community" is again used as an ideological counter to the existing institutions and cultures. In Tönnies and many of the writers of the turn of the century, it was a world that was lost, whose disappearance highlighted the tragic and demeaning character of the modern. In its use in modernization theories, it appears again as a counter-concept—but now as the world to be eradicated, the impediment to the future well-being of the poor. Now Marx and the optimists are the fore-runners, as "modern" and "societal" become glorified. For both periods of intellectual history, the concept has had its ideological usage as a way of critically appraising the existing modes of life; as contrasts between what is and what could be.

Alienation, Mass Society and Community Revisited

In the intellectual world of the twentieth century, the old debate over the disappearance of community and the virtue or evil of the society of organic solidarity has continued to occupy a central place. I shall later discuss the way in which the content of similar terms has undergone change, but the discussion bears much resemblance to that of Durkheim's time.

An aura of pessimism and despair has often marked the usage of the community-society dualism, or its equivalents, in the social scientist's discussions of the present and the future. Sociologists, historians, philosophers and political scientists have mourned the disappearance of a world of tradition, sentiment and loyalty. There is a litany of pathos in the descriptive accounts of the past and present as often presented in contemporary sociological writings.

A great deal of this chorus has utilized assertions of the alienating effects of society, the dehumanizing character of mass society and the search for the re-establishment of communal life as the significant characteristic of modern Western society. Witness the implicit use of the community-society contrast in the following statement from a British historian and demographer:

> The word "alienation" is part of the cant of the mid-twentieth century and it began as an attempt to describe the separation of the worker from his world of work. We need not accept all that this expression has come to convey in order to recognize that it does point to something vital to us all in relation to our past. Time was when the whole of life went forward in the family, in a circle of loved, familiar faces, known and fondled objects, all to human size. That time has gone forever. It makes us very different from our ancestors.[11]

In this chapter I have described the concept "community"

as having a significance in three dimensions. In one dimension it points to and describes a specific form of human association. In another it is part of a theory of change through social evolution. In still a third dimension, it is part of an ideological debate over the value of the present as compared to the past and to possible alternative futures.

This formulation of conceptual dimensions sets the outline of the remaining chapters: three problems form their substance.

First, how usable is "community" and the contrast conception of "community and society" in understanding human association?

Second, how usable is the social evolutionary theory of "community and society" in understanding social change in the contemporary world of industrial and developing nations?

Third, how is the "community-society" contrast used in the present dialogue and debate assessing modern life and its worth?

Notes to Chapter 1

[1] I disagree with Robert Nisbet in his contention (*Social Change in History*) that the evolutionary theorists of the nineteenth century saw change as continuous. Not only is the Marxian theory of revolution difficult to fit into this contention. It is further belied by the extent to which these writers believed that the events of their century had made a distinctive and qualitative change in the character of human life; not commensurate with other centuries.

[2] Robert Nisbet, *The Sociological Tradition*, New York and London, 1966; p. 57.

[3] Émile Durkheim, *The Division of Labor in Society* (3rd Edition, 1902) trans. by George Simpson, Glencoe, Illinois and London, 1947; p. 129.

[4] Max Weber, *Theory of Social and Economic Organization*, trans. by A. M. Henderson and Talcott Parsons, New York and London, 1947; p. 136.

[5] Max Black, *Models and Metaphors*, Ithaca, New York, 1962; p. 229.

[6] Max Weber, *The Methodology of the Social Sciences*, trans. and edited by Edward A. Shils and Henry Finch, Glencoe, Illinois and London, 1949.

[7] Reinhard Bendix and Bennett Berger, "Images of Society and Problem of Concept Formation in Sociology" in Llewellyn Gross, ed., *Symposium on Sociological Theory*, Chicago, 1959; p. 101.

8 Émile Durkheim, *Suicide*, trans. by John A. Spaulding and George Simpson, orig. published in 1897. Glencoe, Illinois and London, 1951; p. 388.

9 Ibid., p. 378.

10 Center for International Studies, Massachusetts Institute of Technology; *Report to the United States Senate Committee on Foreign Relations* (*Study No. 12*), 1960. Reprinted in Claude Welch, Jr. (ed.) *Political Modernization* (Belmont, California: Wadsworth Publishing Company, Inc., 1967), p. 36.

11 Peter Laslett, *The World We Have Lost*, New York and London, 1965; p. 21.

2

THE SOCIAL CONSTRUCTION
OF COMMUNITY

Concepts as Existential Types

Introduction

Where shall we look for community in contemporary human associations? Can we distinguish some human aggregations that are communal and some that are societal? Modern social organization, as Durkheim pointed out, is composed of a multitude of different and diverse groups, organizations, subcultures, and associations. Since our concepts denote a quality of human relations rather than a quantity of population, we need to describe the kind of social bond existing both *within* the groups and associations of a society and *between* them. We are members of families, neighborhoods, occupational organizations, nations, churches. We act and interact with others who may share those affiliations and with others who share none of them.

A joke provides us with the introduction for this chapter. The story is told of a dying Jew who in his last hour asks to be converted to Christianity. His sons plead against it but the old man wins out, is converted and given the last rites of the Church. The children cannot understand why their father, always a devout and Orthodox Jew, should renounce his lifelong faith and they prevail on him to explain. With his dying breath the old man rises up in bed and shouts, "Better one of *them* should die than one of *us*."

Two aspects of this story are useful for this chapter. The

first is the *exclusivity* of the old man's loyalties. The distinction he has drawn between *"them and us"* is a sharp one. The sentiment of being one of *us* is too emotional for explanation or justification on grounds of rational self-interest. It is intrinsic and in this sense self-evident to those within its context. That is why the children cannot understand the old man's willingness to become one of *them!* It is precisely because the father has been the embodiment of communal sentiment that his death-bed conversion seems so "out of character." The humor comes when we realize how the dying Jew has remained consistent and resolved our paradox. He dies still within the communal fold.

The second aspect of significance is found in the father's attempt to define himself as something other than what he has been—to create communal membership through *symbolic construction.* It is funny and inappropriate in this context, yet it points to the question of how it is that people do identify themselves and others as belonging to one or another association. By symbolic construction we refer to a process of creating and signifying the existence and character of persons and objects by the ways in which human beings conceptualize, talk about and define them. This process is emphasized in the discussion of how it is that associations and relationships come to be seen as communal or societal by the acting members of society.

Concepts as Existential Types

It is necessary to understand that the actor—the person studied by the observer—has the same problem of interpreting experience as does the observer. The flux and fluidity of the real world can neither be grasped nor communicated in its multiple, infinite form. But it is neither perceived nor talked about in such naive, pristine fashion. Instead, experience is made up out of selected aspects of the empirical realities and perceived through the aid of ideal-types, such as statuses, roles and other patterns.

The actor then operates in some respects as does the sociologist: through the use of ideal-types which enable him to experience reality in a naive fashion, taking for granted the character of a reality actually constructed; that is, formed out of perceptions and typifying procedures which create and impose a selection and orderliness on the flow of realities. Whether a given set of events and relationships are approached by the actor as communal or societal cannot be given to the observer by the character of the object—the activities which involve the parties—but are created as the parties define the situation as one that is for them communal or societal.

The sociologist is then two steps removed from the realities of the world. No matter how he may define or discuss a given event or situation, the operative aspects of it will be designated by the selection and definition of the actors. Theirs are the *existential types*—those used in the process of living. The famous statement of W. I. Thomas is here appropriate: "If men define a situation as real, it is real in its consequences."[1] The sociologist, in observing human behavior, is studying ideal-types at a secondary stage—as *scientific types*. The objects of study—such as communal or societal groups—are constructed and constituted by the actors; they do not have an independent existence. It is in this sense that the commonsense, everyday actions of people can be conceived as methodologies for gaining and using knowledge.[2]

The implication of these ideas is that in order to analyze these concepts, we must discuss how it is that members of the society come to typify experiences as communal, societal or otherwise.

Communal Identity and Solidarity

The usages of "community" that have been discussed may be seen as deriving meaning for the actors in social situations as contrasts in somewhat the same sense that the community-society distinction involves contrasts for the social scientist analyzing the situation. They constitute appeals to persons to behave in specified ways because they are members of a community of people who have particular claims on each other that others do not have. "You and I are not strangers but are part of the same community and therefore should act differently than we each would toward strangers." The appeal is to a common identity and to rules of solidarity.

Asserting communal ties takes the interaction out of one setting and places it in a different context of rules. Among the Mafia in the United States, for example, claims of loyalty and mutual help rested on the designation of common kinship and common ethnicity-Italian. Even the use of fictive kinship-godfatherhood-provided a similar appeal. It is noteworthy that appeals to common membership and communal feelings so often use the language of kinship—"the brotherhood" among Negroes, "sisters" in the Woman's Liberation Movement, "fraternity brothers" on college campuses.

A comparison of communal appeals with other noncommunal types may make the point clearer. The concept of 'class" presents an almost "pure" form of societal group. The processual aspect of "class" emerges in Marx's distinction between "class in itself" and "class for itself." A "class in itself" is *not* an organized group of associates; it is an analytical category, such as "bourgoisie," (owners of the means of production) used by observers to describe and analyze society. It becomes a "class for itself" when organization develops and a self-consciousness emerges among members that they are class members and they come to act collectively toward mutual class goals. "Class consciousness" is part of the group but the individual's relation to class aims are those of his mutual interests with other class members and not with the class aims as an intrinsic end. The mutual interest of the class members are realized through class organization as in labor unions, and political parties.

In the flux of events, we need to emphasize that any given association of people *may*, under given circumstances, take on communal *or* societal aspects as its primary ones. Thus the dominant bond among family members *can* be the aggregation and maintenance of property, and in many societies, classes and historical periods it has been. Here rational interests provide the source of much of the integration and loyalty of members. Similarly, an economic class *may* act communally, cherish its styles of life and develop strong intrinsic sentiments. Appeals to upper-class identity or to proletarian community are efforts to construct such groups on bases other than similarity of economic interests. Empirically, appeals to both interests and sentiments may operate at the same time in the same group.

Primordial Groups

The emergence of new national units in Asia and Africa following World War II and the retreat of colonial powers has focused much attention on efforts of new governments to promote and develop a consciousness of nationhood. With this perspective, pre-existent attachments to regional, local and cultural groups have been viewed as potentially detrimental to the formation of national identities. Tribe, region, kin, caste and religion are seen as creating loyalties and affiliations which clash with conceptions of oneself as member of a nation. In a salient paper, "The Integrative Revolution: Primordial Sentiments and Civil Politics in the New States," Clifford Geertz refers to these sources of group loyalty as "primordial":

By a primordial attachment is meant one that stems from the givens of social existence, immediate contiguity and kin mainly, but beyond them the givenness that stems from being born into a particular religious community, speaking a particular language . . . and following particular social practices. These congruities are seen to have an ineffable, and at times, overpowering *coerciveness in and of themselves.* [Italics mine—JG] One is bound to one's kinsman, one's neighbor, one's fellow believer, *ipso facto* as the result not merely of personal affection, practical necessity common interest or incurred obligation, but at least in great part by virtue of some unaccountable absolute impact attributed to the very tie itself.[3]

Insofar as such "primordial groups" generate intensive loyalties they may take precedence over national loyalties and diminish the force of national affiliations. In 1962, when Chinese and Indian troops fought in the Himalayas, many Indian governmental and intellectual leaders were gratified and surprised that the patriotic response seemed as strong in South India, far from the battles, as in Northern India. A common conception of "us" as including all Indian citizens appeared to be developing. Against this, Indian history since Independence has been marked by continuous struggles of linguistic, religious and regional groups to develop degrees of political identity and autonomy from the national center.

In a somewhat similar concern, Max Weber referred to this primacy of the primordial group in contrast to relations with other groups as a form of "dual ethic"—the use by the same person of a communal ethic of sentiment in relationships with some groups but an ethic of unrestrained self-interest with other groups. Such duality can be illustrated in Edward Banfield's study of a Southern Italian village reported in *The Moral Basis of a Backward Society* (1958). Banfield observed the absence of sentiments of public welfare among the population, and found instead a ruthless amorality and self-interested character in the individual villager's response to public affairs. At the same time, the villagers displayed strong concerns for the welfare of their family and toward its continuing solidarity. Banfield called this duality a pattern of *amoral familism*. Toward one's kin there is deep sentiment, affection and loyalty; toward those outside of it, there is only naked self-interest. The advancement of the family, rather than the individual or the village, predominates over any other interest or sentiment.

Of course, communal groups have no monopoly on loyalty, obligation, reciprocity or ethical behavior. In Montegrano, the village studied by Banfield, people responded to mutual obligations and expectancies as they did in much of human interaction. What is essential, however, is that these non-familial relationships are expected to occur because they provide a mutual advantage for each party. Motives of self-interest are imputed and appeals to action are couched in those terms. The paesano act toward their fellow men as they see it is to their individual and familial interest to do so and expect a similar logic from others. This was what Durkheim pointed to in speaking of the ties of organic solidarity in modern societies. Within the family, however, a logic of common benefit is both acceptable and anticipated.

The cohesion, glorification and advancement of the communal group is its own *raison d'être*. The appeal to act in the interest of the primordial group has the character of an ultimate end; it need not be legitimated through another principle nor defended by its rational, utilitarian relationship to some other goal. The demands and privileges of community are coercive and self-evident to members, however intricately they may also be involved with self-interest. "My country, may she always be in the right; but right or wrong, my country."

The crucial quality of communal interaction is the recognition that a common identity of communal membership implies special claims which members have on each other, as distinct from others. The coerciveness of such claims have a particularistic character; they include members with no reference to the formal task of the division of labor. Thus E. C. Hughes describes the reluctance of British employers to hire French Canadians for supervisory and executive positions in Quebec in the 1930s. The argument is generally put in this fashion:

> We tried French foremen, but it has not worked out. They pay too much attention to family and friends; the British foreman does his job, is friendly with no one and is just.[4]

D

Community as a Social Construction

In the discussion above we have assumed, as does Geertz in describing the primordial group, that the communal character of an aggregate is "given." That assumption, however, shortcuts a great deal of significant and important analysis. Central to this book is the perspective toward social experience which emphasizes its situational and problematic character. Human beings, in their activities, select out from the manifold potentials of events those which fit their ordered patterns of perception and relate to their interests and purposes. What *is* given is what has come to be perceived and experienced as "given." "The reality of everyday life is taken for granted as reality . . . It is simply there as self-evident and compelling facticity."[5]

This perspective emphasizes the situations in which experience for the actor is conceived as communal or societal rather than the existence of the communal as a *ding an sich* (a thing in itself). When we look for the sources of communal affiliations, our concern is that of process and situation. When do people define themselves as having important characteristics in common, and when do these become bases for communal identity and action?

In the example of nationhood above, we accounted for limits to national commitment by the existence of loyalties which clashed or took precedence over those of the nation; loyalties to groups such as tribe, caste or family. We assumed the reality of the tribe, the caste and the family as social groups. But that reality must itself be accounted for. Consciousness of membership and the corresponding types of appeals to communal sentiment are themselves subjects of analysis and investigation.

Some historians have criticized the sociological usage of "class" to describe a number of pre-industrial situations. They have maintained that, in the perceptions and activities of people in such situations, the concept of "class" did not appear as part of the reality of the actors, either in the use of that term or in other modes of thought. On this basis, in *The Social Interpretation of the French Revolution* (1964), Alfred Cobban has criticized the conception of the French Revolution as a "bourgeois" revolution. Such views of social structure were not those of the actors of the time. Instead, he asserts they are the ways in which the historians and sociologists utilize contemporary perceptions and concerns to build a mythical past and affirm their commitment to a particular impact of the French Revolution as a myth which governs the present. Only with later industrialization do more contemporary usages of "class" emerge in daily life.

It is this perspective that I intend by referring to the social construction of communities. It implies that pre-existing conditions do not, in themselves, "cause" the emergence of community designations. For example, though their language differed from the dominant English, the German immigrants to the United States have lost much of their ethnic separability and self-designation in American political life. They play at most a minor role in American political life. This has not been true for the Irish in America, although language differences from the native American have been slight. Common national origins have not had the same affect on Germans as on Irish in America. The emergence, maintenance, and possible disappearance of such groups is a crucial part of their analysis.

Pre-Conditions of Community

While in this section a number of often suggested pre-conditions for communal development are examined, we recognize that in many circumstances they do not result in communal formation, and under some circumstances, different and even opposite sources can be associated with communal emergence.

A *homogeneous culture* has often been posited as the mark of community. Language, moralities and common histories are expected to produce a sense of being a unique and different people. When meanings and understandings are perceived to be in common, interaction among members is less problematic than with non-members.

Taken in itself, however, common perception does not specify the boundaries of homogeneity. Why don't Europeans develop strong communal ties, since they possess much of common history and customs *as compared* to non-Europeans? Why did American Jews of German origin develop a strong communal identity with American Jews of Russian origin when their "cultures" were *so* opposite? What appear crucial are the situations in which the culture does or does not appear homogeneous; the perception among an aggregate of people that they constitute a community. This "consciousness of kind" is not an automatic product of an abstract "homogeneity."

Another element often cited as productive of communal sentiment is *common territory*. It has so frequently been posited as an essential condition for community that the term is sometimes coterminous with territory, as in the "local community," "community studies," "community power structure." Roland Warren's definition is a case in point: "We shall consider a community to be that combination of social units and systems which perform the major social functions having locality reference."[6] This construction of the object of study in geographical, as well as sociological and psychological terms, leads to studies in urban and rural areas of topics such as ecology, political and functional metropolitanization and the relation between local institutions and those of the wider society. While it constitutes a significant focus of study, it is far removed from the framework of this volume and the kinds of problem which have emerged from the community-society dichotomy and its history.

The use of "community" as a general term for a real territorial settlement, rather than social relationships, has its roots in the tendency to identify the local, small, territorial unit with communal relationships and the large urban and regional units with societal characteristics. Thus village, neighborhood and town appear as seats of community, and interest in their appearance and/or disappearance has been generalized to the wider scope of urban communities, since these constitute the context for the discussion of community change in contemporary societies.

As we are using it here, the concept of community is part of a system of accounts used by members and observers as a way of explaining or justifying the member's behavior. It is the criteria of action that we emphasize rather than the physical arena within which the action occurs. Again, it is the behavior governed by criteria of common belonging rather than mutual interest. An emphasis on the importance of communal affiliation in modern life, which this book advances, implies sharp limits to the principles of rational individual goals and functional roles as cornerstones in the organization and conflicts of contemporary life and society. The description of Montegrano as well as that of other small localities and the existence of nationalistic movements through populations of millions indicate the tenuousness of the geographical sense of community for the problem of this volume. Large territories may be stages for communal bonds (viz. national sentiment) while small territories may be organized on functional bases of rational exchange (viz. Montegrano).

Nevertheless, the relation between territorial size and communalism remains and has continued to be a central issue. The search for a more communal form of existence has often given rise to the emergence of new, small settlements (communes) often operating with the ideology that bigness dilutes community. Here, Redfield's distinction between "folk community" and "urban society" reflects the sense that the city diminishes group ties and promotes just that individualism which Comte, Durkheim and the French conservatives have found so fearful in industrialization, but which others, Bagehot, Marx and Simmel, find an essential part of civilized sophistication.

The "Consciousness of Kind"

This term, first coined by Franklin Giddings (*Studies in the Theory of Human Society* (1922)), expresses the phenomenological perspective which I am using. What are the occasions when the communal affiliation becomes a basis for appeal, for explanation, for adjudication, for the solution of social situations? Marxists refer to class consciousness as the explicit recognition and perception of common interests. In similar usage, communal consciousness emerges in the perception and recognition that "we" have a different set of obligations and rights when acting toward those perceived as part of "our" community than toward those who are seen as outside that community.

The appeal to act as a member of the community, to give special consideration to fellow members, and to place their aims above those of others and of the self must presuppose a recognition of the reality of the community and of the member's affiliation to it. The "consciousness of kind" thus depends on perceiving that there is such a kind and that one is part of it.

Such consciousness is facilitated by the capacity to evoke *symbols of community*. A group name, for example, appears to be an essential part of the development of communal affinity. Teenage gangs abound in naming: "The Young Lords," "The Eagles" or "The Panthers" are all ways of designating exclusivity. At a wider level, we can see a groping toward an expression of community in the emergence of the term "Asian" among Chinese, Japanese and Filipino on American college campuses. When people come into contact with each other, it is through their self-designation and the designation of others in group terms that the situation is defined as an inter-group one and the persons given a standing in group terms. This is especially evident where the situation is capable of emphasizing one or several different statuses, as when a doctor-patient relationship can be conceptualized as one involving a "female doctor," a "doctor," a "Black doctor," or a "female Black doctor." The permutations and combinations ring the many changes of inter-group as compared to inter-role relations.

Within the emergence of a consciousness of kind is the rise of a collective experience; *a sense of participating in the same history.* This, as Milton Gordon describes in discussing ethnic communities, is a way of seeing that "I am ultimately bound up with the fate of this group."[7] Communities might almost be defined as people who see themselves as having a common history and destiny different from others. It is not that communal members participate and associate with each other but that they perceive events and public figures as being involved in their lives, as well as those in face-to-face interaction. That an aggregate of people has a common history ensures the sharing of symbols, legends, names and events that are unlikely to others. "Outsiders" cannot be assumed to know or to care about such matters.

It is even much more than that, however. It also involves shared attitudes toward events, both past and present. Thus, the Asian Indians preserve an antipathy toward Moghul invasions and a pride in having recently defeated the British at cricket. The small town residents in the American Midwest share the memory of the year their high school basketball team won the state tournament. Negroes share the opprobrium of slavery and the pride of resistance and struggle of the civil rights movement and the urban riots.

These considerations make us aware of the importance which history has for communal identity. Independence movements frequently give rise to a cultural "renaissance" in which symbols of group identity are formed and a new history written to provide a prideful past with which to identify. India developed the lion of Ashoka as an ancient symbol; the Irish resurrected Gaelic; the Zionists restored Hebrew. In similar fashion, Negroes have supported and expanded the revision of American history through Black history and Black studies. The reinterpretation of slavery and reconstruction has stressed the role of resistance and competent governing ability in distinction to past historical traditions of Negro passivity and incompetence.

Conflict, Interaction and Communal Identity

Conflict with others and the resulting cooperation and common struggle often provide the experiences from which an aggregate of people develop a sense of themselves as possessed of a common fate and belonging to a common group. "In most communities ... new classifications of human beings develop to coincide with the evolving pattern of differential treatment."[8] Shibutani and Kwan are saying that as people are treated by others as if they were a group they come to perceive themselves as such.

An apt illustration of this process is found in the experience of "the Chinese" in Hawaii. Glick, in his study of immigration into Hawaii (1942), tells us that the migrants from Chinese areas thought of themselves as Cantonese, Pekinese, Northern Chinese or Central Chinese. They had little national consciousness of themselves as sharing a common nationality —Chinese. However, they were treated by the other Hawaiians in the same manner, as a group with a common culture in similar circumstances. That common response from others and their awareness of it brought "the Chinese" into self-consciousness. Regional and local distinctions were gradually lessened in importance and the common features of their backgrounds and racial characteristics increased in their perception of each other in contrast to the non-Chinese. In this sense, they were not Chinese; they became Chinese.

Other groups have gone through similar processes of heightened and lessened communal consciousness. The persecution of the German-Jews during the 1930s and the holacaust of genocide horrified and frightened Jews in many countries of the world. It led to a resurgence of loyalties and unity; a sense of themselves as being Jewish that cut across national, class and religious differences. It was one of the sources of the expansion of the Zionist movement following World War II. In many colonial areas of the world, the independence movements provided the struggle through which was developed the sense of common nationality on which the movement was itself predicated. Independence was sought and justified on a rhetoric of national self-determination while the nation had only a thin existence in the consciousness of many. Some writers, in commenting on current African political problems of dissension and civil war have remarked that, unlike countries such as India, the African countries had not gone through the experience of a long Independence movement. The "nation" had been a convenient expression for colonial administration but the separate regions, tribes, localities, classes, and other groups had not developed a sense of mutual interest or common sentiment about themselves as nation.

The Social Construction of Tradition

The distinction between social groups as symbolic constructions and social groups as objectively given entities is important to the view of community or society as situationally located concepts. The designation or perception of an interaction as involving one form of social bond rather than another is not so much a response to a prearranged set of facts as it is a response to a concrete situation in the present here and now. Even the common fate which I described as one frequent characteristic of communal groups is not something apart from the recognition of it by the group.

I want to illustrate this process—the construction of communal bonds in situated acts—through the analysis of a tradition, a past. Groups are often said to have common traditions. They are often part of the way in which accounts are given to explain behavior by reference to "our tradition." What I am asserting is that such sources of group life are themselves constantly created in situations in which communal categories are salient. People are continuously using a designation of tradition in situations where it is relevant. In doing so, the actors determine what is the tradition and how it comes into play. They "discover" a past hitherto unknown.

The national culture in many new nations is of this character. It has the quality of "rediscovery" of a past previously dormant, ambiguous or non-existent. "... the national culture of every new state is a product of modern manufacture."[9]

The emergence during post-Independence India of Hindi as the historically common language of the people of Northern India illustrates the process by which the present creates the past; people create their peoplehood. Linguists have argued whether or not the various dialects and vocabularies used in areas of Northern India could be designated one language. The large infusion of Urdu (derived from the Persian) in the language of North-Central India, formerly Moslem areas until the eighteenth century, can be contrasted with the use of Sanskrit within the language of North-East India, excluding Bengal. Gandhi favored the development of Hindustani, a mix of the Urdu and the Sanskritized versions. Since Independence the public usages, such as radio and dictionaries, have been heavily affected by literary domination and by political concerns. The public language is thus more Sanskritic than ever. Radio broadcasts of the late 1940s and early 1950s led to complaints of unintelligibility among many "Hindi" listeners. In one part of Hindi-speaking Bihar, the Maithili are struggling to retain their group designation of their language (Maithili) and to resist its characterization as a form of Hindi (Brass). The Hindi language was not "revived." It was defined and even created as people in specific social locations facing specific immediate situations decided what it had been. The process is not one of discovery but of composition.

This process is by no means peculiar to India. In the United States, some Blacks are consciously seeking to redefine certain modes of speaking English, previously derogated as "Black English" and thus revalue it as accepted and usable, an object of pride rather than shame. In this process the forms of speech once seen as illogical or unintelligible are now found to be adequate as grammar and as logical, given the experiences of its speakers (Labov). This process also leads to the recognition that much which passes as "traditional" has emerged only in the recent past and has quickly become embedded in group history. The "traditional" role of the Japanese Emperor as the source of national loyalties dates from the Meiji Restoration of 1868 and the "traditional" Jim Crow segregation laws of the American South date from the late 1890s.

The Problem of Group Existence

This emphasis on process rather than structure in the analysis of human associations gives us a view of associational designations that is more fluid and flexible than that presented in the evolutionary stages of Durkheim or Tönnies. The nature of the social bond and the selection of bondsmen is not a fixed and given fact; a part of the *essence* of a group. Instead it is a facet of historical situations; a part of the *existence* of acting persons.

Many social divisions are potentially foci of communal sentiment or of societal interest. The same persons may today select and emphasize their communal attachments; may tomorrow pick and choose their societal complements. The designation of any specific social category as communal by its members or by others is, therefore, not given as an objective fact. It has to be understood within an historical and situational context. Both mechanical and organic solidarity and communal and societal cohesion are constant possibilities; not predetermined features of human associations.

The "group" is itself then a defined and constructed category. We have seen that new groups emerge. It is also the case that old ones disappear as the categorization ceases to be relevant, practical or superseded by others which have become more salient to new situations and contexts. In most contemporary industrial societies, "youth" has emerged as a self-conscious group. That consciousness is both expressed and accentuated in the youth communities to be found in the cities in the special areas of restaurants, lodgings and universities. It is to be found in the development of special markets, such as clothing, magazines and music, that caters for and thus defines youth as a group. In the United States groups such as the "mulatto" and the "Scotch-Irish" have ceased to be socially relevant and the terms are now seldom used. In England the Scottish have by no means disappeared. Neither the mulatto (a person descended from white and Negro ancestors and yellowish-brown in complexion) nor the Scotch-Irish have disappeared as biological types in the United States but their social existence is no longer there. They are no longer "noticed."

Cultural Differences in Group Identification

Since elements of social life which can be perceived as sources of communal identification are themselves problematic. Primordial qualities of lineage or common belief systems may be significant in one culture but may not be as vital in some other culture. Discussions of differences between India and Japan illustrate this point through the diverse meanings which associational membership has in each country.

In her analysis of Japanese society (*Japanese Society*, 1970), the anthropologist Chie Nakane uses an important distinction between *attribute* and *frame* with which to compare India and Japan. In India, caste operates as an attribute of the person which he carries into different arenas. Within a variety of other groups and persons, the attribute of caste membership provides a vital directive for loyalties, limiting and defining a great deal of the caste member's participation in associations, such as school, workplace and residence. In Japan, as Nakane sees it, the units of communal attachment are more likely to include all those engaged in an activity together, operating within a common frame.

Classifications such as landlord and tenant are based on attributes, while such a unit as landlord and his tenants is a group formed by situational position. Taking industry as an example, "lathe operator" or "executive" refers to attribute, but "the members of Y company" refers to frame. In the same way, "professor," "office clerk" and "student" are attributes, whereas "men of Z university" is a frame.[10]

Such considerations are important in recognizing the importance of hierarchy for communal sentiments in India and its lesser salience in Japan. Thus the impact of the educational system on cultural sentiments and on job access is more limited by caste considerations in India than in Japan, where the school provides a system of loyalties with profound ties among all alumni. Japanese trade unionism is largely existent at company level, rather than throughout industry, and even Japanese political interest associations make a strong effort to provide a total agenda of social life for their members (Ishida). In Japan, seemingly associational groups, such as school, political interest group or factories may provide a much stronger sense of communal belonging than is the case in other cultures. In India, caste ties provide similar balances to class diversities, providing a balance of common interest against internal diversities of class, occupation and education.

Pluralistic Arenas

Rather than conceiving of "community" and "society" as groups and/or entities to which persons "belong", it would seem more useful to conceptualize these terms as points of reference brought into play in particular situations and arenas. The individual brings to these situations a plurality of groups, associations and social networks on which he can draw in defining his and other's behavior. The sources of his identifications and the uses to which they are put are derived from the situation as well as from the past affiliations and designations. H. G. Wells has given an amusing and clear sense of this diversity and plurality in writing:

[The botanist] has a strong feeling for systematic botanists as against plant physiologists, whom he regards as lewd and evil scoundrels in this relation; but he has a strong feeling for all botanists, and indeed all biologists, as against physicists, and those who profess the exact sciences, all of whom he regards as dull, mechanical, ugly-minded scoundrels, in this relation; but he has a strong feeling for all who profess what he calls Science, as against psychologists, sociologists, philosophers and literary men, whom he regards as wild, foolish, immoral scoundrels in this relation; but he has a strong feeling for all educated men as against the working man, whom he regards as a cheating, lying, loafing, drunken, thievish, dirty scoundrel in this relation; but so soon as the working man is comprehended together with these others, as *Englishmen*, he holds them superior to all sorts of Europeans, whom he regards. . . .[11]

In the highly pluralistic societies of the modern world, the individual can now stress one community rather than another or can focus attention on the associational interests binding him to otherwise conflicting communities. The same person is at once a Catholic, a student, a lawyer, a woman, an American. Each definition brings different loyalties and purposes into play.

Citizens of one country have often experienced a clear sense of their national membership only when living in another country. Even sophisticated intellectuals, contemptuous of patriotic feeling, openly critical of their national culture and condemning ideals of national solidarity have remarked on their surprising surge of fellow-feeling toward those who share their language and their "territory" when they find themselves in a foreign country where others define them as Americans, or French, or British.

Levels of Community

Anthropologists have faced this conceptual problem as they have become aware that it is unwarranted to view peasant and even primitive settlements today as if they were isolated, self-sufficient establishments. Travel, the importation of goods, the appearance of jobs, governmental rules and welfare services—all these are only a small sample of the processes which diminish the uniqueness, exclusivity and isolation of the "folk society" and make it essential to describe the territorial community as part of a larger societal whole.

Theories and concepts which posit levels of integration and/or participation view the individual and/or the group as participating in different institutional complexes. The idea of levels is that of steps, each of which includes a set of lesser "communities;" family-village-tribe-region-nation. (A little like the child's address as self, home town, state, nation, hemisphere, world, solar system, and universe.) At each level there are sets of persons and institutions which require different kinds of behavior and affect the person or community "beneath" it in different ways. Each level, however, includes those below.

It is important to recognize that these relationships are by no means similar at each level, even within the territorial patterns. Some are structural and more purely societal than others—as in the Indian villager's use of governmental medical facilities, either through services offered in the village by visiting clinics or by traveling to a nearby city for their use. One cannot explain the medical institution of the "community" without reference to these extra-village activities, but they do not involve a sense of common primordial or communal membership. On the other hand, there are those groups in which the person and the local settlement can feel membership and ties of loyalty—such as a nation, a race, a linguistic group—but which occupy less than immediate territorial ties. Robert Redfield, commenting on Evans-

Pritchard's study of the African tribe of the Nuer, describes just such a situation:

> ... the community of "my people" is subdivided into a whole series of communities inclosed within one another and characterized by a transition from intimate relations and functions and from domestic institutions to less intimate relations and functions and to political institutions.[12]

In the same section, Redfield makes another distinction of importance between those the Nuer regard as "my people" and other groups with whom they interact but who are traditional enemies, and those who are alien yet impinge on the life of the Nuer—the British colonial government being the most significant.

Arenas of Situated Action

The rigid use of the "community-society" typology is a basic flaw in this conception of levels of territory in describing modern societies. In posing the "little community" against the "great society" anthropologists influenced by Redfield's work have continued to minimize the existence of communal ties in the wider areas of region, metropolis, nation, and even the world. This body of work has been extremely valuable in demonstrating the diversity of culture which differentiates the local and provincial of the village from that of the cosmopolitan and national level. But in suggesting that wider levels involve a diminution of bonds based on primordial and communal ties, they are misleading. The difficulty lies in thinking of communities as fixed social groups rather than as processes; in conceiving of institutions as clusters of values and normative procedures rather than as arenas in which people are acting to achieve purpose.

In describing and analyzing peasant societies, Redfield was quite clear that it was insufficient to use the concept of an isolable society in the same way as could be done with primitive tribes, at least in the past generation. The ties that united the villager in peasant societies to wider social units emerge both within and without the village, linking the village to wider systems of social relationships. While some of those relationships are less personal, more interest-oriented and exchange-like in character, others are extensions of communal, sentimental ties of family and group. In India, for example, the residents of a specific village often have a large number of relations by marriage and/or by caste in many villages within the region or even in the metropolis. They create bonds which can be used in crises, sometimes for information and sometimes for sociability.

The role of familial, caste, ethnic and other communal ties is an important factor in the way people use seemingly societal institutions. The integration of the villager into the district, the region or the nation is not effected exclusively through mechanisms of societal character, in which personal interest and economic exchange govern his relationships. Wider communities are forged through the extension of local communities into urban and sub-regional arenas and through the appearance of new communal groups in new situations. Tribal, caste and ethnic formulations serve as significant means by which the urban migrant, in many societies, finds his attachments in an otherwise anonymous settlement. He can call upon people with whom he has no prior personal acquaintance but who are joined through common member-ship in a community of an ethnic, religious, caste or other group whose consciousness of themselves as a communal category provides him with an existent relationship. He has a ready-made membership as "one of us." Even the economic exchange relationship in developing areas makes much use of such bonds of sentiment in providing the essential ingredients of trust for economic trade.

Communal Networks

The loose character of these relationships is not caught firmly in the net of the concept of "group." That implies

E

more definitiveness and persistence of persons and inter-
actions than is the case. J. B. Barnes' concept of "social networks" provides a better tool for describing the relation of
the little community to larger areas. In his study of a
Norwegian parish (1954) Barnes found it necessary to consider social ties which are not readily subsumable by the
concept of "group." In Bremnes, the village Barnes studied,
residents belonged to many groups—households, hamlets,
wards, parishes. "At different times and different places
membership in one or another group is definitive for what he
does." The fishermen's group became salient in fishing but
did not extend into other areas of life. The individual can be
seen as acting within a field, or arena, in which his behavior
is specific and situational.

Barnes delineated three such fields—the *territorial*, in
which the persons related to others in interaction based on
his physical settlement; the *industrial*, where conflict and
cooperation emerged within meanings and definitions
attuned to the needs and purposes of fishing vessels and
marketing cooperatives; and *social networks*, made up of ties
of friendship, kinship and acquaintance.

A network of this kind has no external boundary, nor has
it any clear-cut internal divisions, for each person sees
himself at the center of a collection of friends.[18]

Such networks connect persons to each other as points on a
line; generating relationships which intersect and reach both
within and between parishes. These networks are not groups
in the sense of a lasting organization with sharp definitions
of exclusivity and inclusiveness.

In my analysis of social arenas the emphasis is on the coexistence of both communal and societal reference points.
The "arena," as a concept, lacks the definiteness and normative character of "institution." For our discussion, what is
crucial is that such networks are capable of being used as
points of reference out of which particular relations can be
called upon for specific arenas of action. The Indian villager,

with a network of friends growing out of the marriages of his kin, can utilize these in his travels, even though the individual members of the network are unknown to him. The Japanese member of a university can use the ties established by common university background and call on alumnae he has never met to provide him with privileges. Such networks lack the stability and diffuseness of social groups but their situated quality is nevertheless utilized for communal relations, albeit only in specific circumstances. Elizabeth Bott, in *Family and Social Network* (1957), has used a somewhat similar idea in conceptualizing "class" as a point of reference used by members for particular kinds of actions and specific arenas of activity. Rather than perceiving of "class" as a group, she utilized it as a term of references by which social members organize and categorize specific situations.

These considerations provide a basis for understanding how communal points of reference emerge in modern societies without the kind of territorial and interpersonal experiences often seen as essential to the development and persistence of community. Communal networks, bonds and groups can and do function in a wider ambit, alongside the societal levels and relationships. The coexistence of both as points of reference makes the outcome of change highly dependent on the complexities of specific situations. The nuclear family, for example, is seen by many sociologists as a significant element in the development of a class structure because it maximizes mobility and enables the individual to follow the dictates of economic opportunities, unhampered by the demands of extended kin. On the other hand, the extended kin can persist within the structure of class-oriented mobility, held together by occasional visits, phone calls and letters. Even though not in daily interaction, the capacity to call on the extended kin in moments of crisis, to use it as a network for social and economic aid and for historic continuity remains strong in modern societies. Viewed as a social network, capable of mobilization, the extended family appears quite salient and useful in modern life, even though quite distinct from the kinship group as a localistic structure.

Modern Society: The Widened Dimensions of Community

The growth of large-scale political organization, of national and international economic markets, of intensive specialization and extensive communications has not spelled the demise of the communal impulse. Not only do communal groups persist and emerge in modern life, but they often proliferate into wider and more extensive groups, functioning on a broader scale and operating in broader arenas.

The fate of ethnicity in the United States is one apt illustration of the tendency for communal ties to extend along wider lines. In the 1920s, sociologists observing the immigration of the early 1900s in the United States and the patterns of institutional life among immigrants loudly proclaimed the coming of "the melting pot;" they prophesied the assimilation, if not amalgam, of immigrant cultures into a new joint product or, at least, the disappearance of distinctive immigrant ways of life and separability and their replacement by a dominant white, Protestant and nativist American ethos. The prediction has not been realized, least of all in the large urban areas where it was most expected. The Irish, the Poles, the Slavics, the Italians, the Jews have by no means lost their identity, their separateness, their social institutions, their visibility or their political leadership. In addition, newer ethnic and racial groups—the Puerto Ricans, the Mexican-Americans, the Negroes—have entered the big cities and continue the pluralistic character of American urban cultures.

Similarly, and relatedly, the religious differences in American life have persisted to reinforce ethnic diversities. While intermarriage between major religious groups is more frequent, it is far from eradicating the communal distinctions between Catholics, Protestants and Jews. In fact, the nature and process of real estate development in American cities has served to perpetuate and accentuate ethnic and racial differences, as suburbs take on distinctive communal character.

It is not only that ethnic groups in the United States have

remained as discrete social organizations. They have persisted in retaining and even reinforcing their character as foci of social cohesion and solidarity, in national and regional arenas as well as on local levels. (As I argue in Chapter 3, such qualities of ethnic loyalty have been useful in achieving and maintaining advantages in the division of labor and in politics.) While "ticket balancing" has been a blatant and visible testimony to the ethnic character of America's largest city, New York, the role of ethnic and racial communalism has been salient in many areas of American political life. Since the rise of the Black civil rights and power movements, the search for ethnic identities and organization has been even more self-conscious and explicit. The role of communal consciousness and solidarity in national politics has persisted and remains a salient facet of American voting patterns.

The persistence and accentuation of such primordial cohesion cannot be understood as a continuation of primary group, face-to-face, interaction. Politically and culturally American ethnic groups are national, as well as state and regional in character. Their heroes are built up in a national communications net; their organizations are centralized and operate at national levels. The Italian in New Jersey responds to many of the same communal events as the Italian in San Francisco. People who do not know each other nevertheless see themselves in the same category and share the same friends and enemies. A figure such as the Spanish-American Reyes Tijerina welded both the Spanish-Americans and the Mexican-Americans more firmly into a common ethnic group through the national reports of his actions. These are communities that operate as much on a national as on a local plane.

The very acceptance of the language and paradigm of American communalism reinforces its existence. It enables non-members to continue to interpret events as accountable by reference to ethnic sentiments and to organize their own actions around such interpretations. Glazer and Moynihan, in their study of ethnicity in New York City, have pointed out that the terms in which the politician makes sense of the city and tries to capture power give prominence to ethnic and communal traits. The social organization of the city admits and accepts ethnicity and this also permits and supports its continuation:

> Ethnicity is more than an influence on events; it is commonly the source of events. Social and political institutions do not merely respond to ethnic interests; a great number of institutions exist for the specific purpose of serving ethnic interests. This in turn tends to perpetuate them. In many ways the atmosphere of New York City is hospitable to ethnic groupings; it recognizes them and rewards them and to that extent encourages them.[14]

The process of widening and increasing the scope and size of communal groups is further illustrated in India, where the primordial ties of caste have by no means disappeared with Independence or with political egalitarianism through elections. On the contrary the widening of political and economic units of social organization through development of the nation-state, the national market and the increased participation of various social levels in political life has stimulated the development of caste organization along broader, more regional and national lines. Local sub-castes (jatis) have been uniting with each other into larger aggregations. Mass communications and electoral politics have made such fusion both possible and advantageous. Here, too, occasions for public designations provide opportunities for group emergence. When the 1901 Census undertook to inventory and classify Indian castes, there was pressure on the Census Department to provide new status positions for old castes and to legitimate new names and definitions to old castes. In this way, as also in the last such Census of caste—1931—the Census, a rational, societal mechanism, was enlisted in the traditional procedures of communal mobility. Even where old caste lines are breaking down, new communal groups are being formed through sub-caste intermarriages. Wider forms of endogamy are coming into existence. Especially among the highly educated occupational and governmental elites, such processes are producing new castes rather than destroying the criteria of caste.

Similarly, the Indian experience in the past two decades has shown a growing incorporation of village and local peoples into more regional and wider linguistic cultures. The occurrence of regional educational centers for high schools and colleges has stimulated the production of regional literary and artistic cultural products and the deliberate formulation of linguistic and regional "nationalism": ". . . linguistic regionalism has been given a new importance by modern developments. What were mainly observer's regions of classification have increasingly become a participant's regions of classification."[15]

The theorists of social evolution had stressed the impact of an extended division of labor on human associations. They had prophesied the decline of social groups and settlements where the sources of cohesion came from principles of social similarity. In their writing they saw a future world in which mutual interest and rational exchange replaced kinship feeling and sentiments of collective membership; where common economic function and occupational specialization served as the major seed-bed of social cohesion *within* groups while complementary needs and exchange provided for continuing relations *between* groups. In this chapter, I have presented many instances in which the communal impulse and the communal groups, independent of role in the division of labor, continue to perform as active and significant features of modern life.

The perspective I have taken here, however, suggests that the evolutionary theorists adopted a narrowed and fixed view of social objects. They saw them as, in Durkheim's term, "social facts," exterior to and impinging on the person as fixed and stable objects; once we begin to think about social groups as a process of selection, construction and creation by acting people we introduce a less preordained, "inevitable" and determined view of human action. Associational life contains a greater possibility of ambiguity, coexisting differences and flexible change. Having seen the fluidity of the concepts themselves, we can begin to discuss the underlying principles of social change which evolutionary theory has utilized in discussing the present and the future.

Notes to Chapter 2

1 Originally stated by W. I. Thomas in *The Unadjusted Girl.*

2 This is what those sociologists labelled "ethnomethodologists" are doing in studying human behavior through the prism of "folk" methods for constructing reality. See especially Harold Garfinkel, *Studies in Ethnomethodology,* Englewood Cliffs, New Jersey, 1967.

3 Clifford Geertz, "The Integrative Revolution" in Geertz, ed., *Old Societies and New States,* Glencoe, Illinois, 1963; p. 109.

4 Everett C. Hughes, *French-Canada in Transition,* Chicago, 1963; p. 55.

5 Peter Berger and Thomas Luckmann, *The Social Construction of Reality,* New York and London, 1966; p. 25.

6 Roland Warren, *The Community in America,* New York, 1963; p. 9.

7 Milton M. Gordon, *Assimiliation in American Life,* New York, 1964; p. 53.

8 Tamotsu Shibutani and Kiankwan, *Ethnic Stratification,* New York, 1965; p. 202.

9 Kim Marriott, "Cultural Policy in the New States" in Geertz, op. cit., p. 56.

10 Chie Nakane, *Japanese Society,* Berkeley, California, 1970; p. 2.

11 H. G. Wells, *A Modern Utopia,* p. 322. Quoted by Robert Bierstedt in *The Social Order,* New York, 1970; p. 294.

12 Robert Redfield, *Peasant Society and Culture,* Chicago, 1956; p. 119.

13 J. B. Barnes, "Class and Committees in a Norwegian Island Parish," *Human Organization,* VII (Feb., 1954). Quoted from reprinted version in Robert French, ed., *The Community,* F. E. Peacock Publishers Inc., 1969; p. 129.

14 Nathan Glazer and Daniel Moynihan, *Beyond the Melting Pot,* Cambridge, Mass., 1963; p. 310.

15 David Mandelbaum, *Society in India,* Volumes I and II, Berkeley, California, 1970; Vol. II, p. 400.

3

COMMUNITY *IN* SOCIETY
Concepts as Systems

Introduction

The evolutionary theorists of social change perceived the world in motion from one type of social organization to another. They sought the dominant modes of organization which characterized stages in the development and history of mankind. A similar perspective has emerged in recent years as sociologists have responded to the plethora of new nations and the issues of economic development and political change which have occurred in this post-colonial era. The analysis of the modernization perspective reveals how the community-society contrast has again been used in an evolutionary scheme.

Modernization theories arose in the process of attempting to predict, understand and prescribe social and political changes requisite to economic growth in the new nations and newly developing areas of the world, particularly following World War II. With many individual qualifications, theorists have used the distinction between community and society and the evolutionary theory of change it embodied. Much of this is reflected in the contrast between the traditional and the modern. Like the conceptualization of community and society, the relationship between tradition and modernity is that of a zero-sum game; the more modernity, the less tradition. Like community and society the traditional and the modern constitute two systems of interrelated and interdependent ideal-types. *The traditional society* is contrasted with *the modernized society*. Lastly, an evolutionary progression is postulated; developing societies are moving in a direction away from the traditional and converging toward development into modern society.

Concepts as Systems

I use the idea of system to characterize the concepts of "community and society" and "tradition and modernity" because of two aspects which they display. First, these are encompassing or umbrella-like terms which sum up, or collate, a variety of other parts of social change. Thus they become implicated in theories of stratificational change, of cultural change, of religious change, of institutional and cultural change in general. Each includes a set of concepts making up an organization of concepts into a system. Secondly, each concept treats a type of social organization as a social system; that is, as a set of mutually interdependent and consistent parts whose character and functioning is interrelated. As such, the contrasting concept is not only logically opposite; it is in conflict. "Community" must decline if "society" is to grow. "Tradition" and "modernity" are in struggle and one must give way to the advantage of the other.

Wilbert Moore has expressed the point of this contrast as it is used in the theory of modernization:

What is involved in modernization is a "total" transformation of a traditional or pre-modern society into the types of technology and associated social organization that characterizes the "advanced", economically prosperous and relatively politically stable nations of the Western World. Because so many aspects of the social order in the underdeveloped areas of the world do not conform with the models set by the advanced countries, there is room for improvement in practically any direction one looks. . . . The ultimate goal: a general transformation in the way life is socially organized.[1]

What I assert in this chapter is that this use of the community-society dichotomy as a theory of social evolution distorts and confuses processes of social change. By utilizing the image of system and systemic relationships, the openness and flexibility of alternatives available to human action is understated and narrowed. The persistence and continuation of communal elements and the emergence of societal institutions and activities are not *necessarily* in conflict. Experience in contemporary changing societies forces the sociologist into a less dualistic view of social change and into a less evolutionary and less rigid perspective. We can better understand change by emphasizing the mixture and interpenetration of types than we can by emphasis on conflict between systems.

Community in Stratification Theory

I will move into the discussion of modernization theories of social change by analyzing the use of the community-society dualism in theories of social stratification. This serves two purposes. First, it demonstrates how the dualism of nineteenth-century evolutionary theory became linked to contemporary theories as part of a system of social stages. Second, it also concentrates attention on a central point of contemporary evolutionary theory: the importance of the division of labor and class development in producing the system of changes characterizing modern societies.

Central to theories of social stratification has been the proposition that communal ties are inimical to social structures in which achievement, performance and mobility are frequent and legitimate. Kinship, neighborhood, ethnicity, race and the other ascriptive sources of community are seen as impediments to the development of fluid social structures and to the emergence of classes. In this fashion the evolutionary models of Durkheim arise, like the phoenix, from the ashes of nineteenth-century social theory.

In the discussion of social stratification it has been customary for sociologists to distinguish between systems of caste and systems of class or, in more general terms, between closed and open systems. The estates of medieval France or the caste structures of India have been cited as the epitome of "closed" systems. Here ascribed qualities of birth determined the social and economic power and privilege of the individual; mobility was rare and unsanctioned and the boundaries between social levels were clearly perceived and often underlined by formal divisions. The concept of class structure is used as a contrast; an open system in which mobility is both possible and sanctioned; individualistic criteria of achievement and merit, independent of birth, are used to legitimate social differences and the boundaries between units—classes—are unclear and difficult to perceive.

Another aspect of this distinction is the perception of the transition from closed to open systems of stratification as an individualizing process. Closed systems are seen as binding the person and his destiny to that of his community, while open systems provide a basis for change in individual status, uninfluenced by one's family, race, or other group membership. One sociologist, André Beteille, writing about modern India, describes it in the context of closed and open stratification in this way:

> This kind of movement, however, where a caste is the unit of mobility, is very different from that which is becoming increasingly common in modern India. The latter allows greater scope to the individual as the unit of mobility and tends increasingly to relegate caste to a marginal position.[2]

This distinction, between groups or individuals as the basic units of stratification, is a major issue in stratification theory. Those who have been preoccupied with the measurement and prediction of social mobility have tended to emphasize the individual and have paid little attention (with the exception of racial categories) to the ways in which entire groups rise or fall. Beteille's remarks above were made in the context of India, where the unit of analysis has so often been the group in which this correction was necessary.

The distinction is significant as well because it poses the community-society dichotomy in another framework; that of the division of labor. Here Durkheim's contrasts are influential. The communal groups are not solely functional, task-related aspects of economy. In ascription, in their historical identity and in their social solidarity they differ from classes, whose relationship to the economic market is their essential point of definition.

In this manner, the construction of the object of stratification, the unit to be studied, already carries with it a theory of stratification—a set of assertions about what is changing and how it is changing.

Community and Society in Marx and Weber: Class and Status

In any discussion of stratification theory, the influence of Karl Marx and of Max Weber must be recognized. The impact of evolutionary theory on Marx is clear and has been touched on earlier. While Weber was by no means as clearly an evolutionary thinker, the conceptions of social hierarchy which he introduced have become part of modern views of change. The distinction between "class" and "status" has had implications for analogous but more encompassing concepts of the modern and the traditional.

Karl Marx's concept of class has two sides to it. In one usage, classes are defined "objectively," by their common economic activities and power, from the standpoint of the observer. Such a social unit lacks the shared perspectives, common culture, formal organization, or sense of belonging that are the stuff of social groups, communal or societal. This is a class "an sich" (in itself)—not conscious of its character or its interests. In another Marxian usage, the "class for itself" (für sich) is an aggregate of people who share common economic and political interests by virtue of similar placement in the economy. This is a group conscious of itself and organized as a class with specific interests and with a consensus about its political enemies.

Much of Marxist politics is concerned with transforming the class *in itself* ("an sich") into a class *for itself* ("für sich"). Much of Marxist social analysis is a demonstration of the logic of this political analysis:

> The economic conditions have in the first place transformed the mass of the people of the country into wage workers. The domination of capital has created for this mass of people a common situation with common interests. Thus the mass is already a class, as opposed to capital, but not yet for itself. In the struggle ... this mass unites, it is constituted as a class for itself. The interests which it defends are the interests of its class.[3]

For the Marxist political parties, revolutionary organizations and trade unions are all potential class-conscious groups. These are societal groups for whom mutual interests are the bond of social solidarity. Whether or not other elements of communal attachment exist is peripheral to the logic of class formation, although of importance tactically. It is the economic position which will dominate political action. Common lineage, territorial origins, ethnicity, race, religion, sex and other bonds of group identity are irrelevant to the economic experience; in the long run they are politically insignificant.

The perspective of Max Weber toward social stratification is a criticism of this singlistic analysis of social strata. For Marx the only significant form of social hierarchy is the class structure. For Weber there are separate orders or dimensions of stratification. Sometimes they are independent of each other; sometimes reinforcing; often they are in conflict. While classes are defined by their economic position, their "life chances on the market," "status groups," are not just economic classes in another form. The two are not different levels of the same bases for social membership. For Weber, both propertied and propertyless people might belong to the same status group. The economic order involves the distribution of material goods; the social order involves the distribution of honor or prestige. Organized classes are societal associations of mutual interests. Status groups are communities with common styles of life.

It is in the context of this discussion of class and status that Weber again defines the community-society dualism: "Communal action refers to that action which is oriented to the feeling of actors that they belong together. Societal action, on the other hand, is oriented to a rationally motivated adjustment of interests."[4] The distinction is again used in Weber's view of status groups as communities. Concern for the preservation and enhancement of social honor is part of the demand for a specific life style incumbent on members and the character of status groups makes for exclusive criteria of membership different from economic or occupational categories. Classes are not communities although they *may* be possible bases for communal action.

Caste, Class and Social Class: The Flow of Stratification

For both Marx and Weber, the units of stratification were relatively discrete. Neither economic roles nor status boundaries shaded off into each other. Hence a transformation from one *system* of stratification to another was analytically feasible. The distinction between communal units and societal units could be utilized in sociological analysis, since the distinctions between classes or between class and status referred to empirical differences.

Beginning with the work of W. Lloyd Warner in the United States during the late 1930s and increasingly in the research and writings of European and Japanese scholars, sociologists have been developing a "half-way" house of communal and societal elements in order to describe the social stratification of modern, industrialized societies, both capitalist and socialist. The concept of "social class" emerged in an attempt to define the character of empirically discoverable groups.

By class is meant two or more orders of people who are believed to be, and are accordingly ranked by the members of the community, in socially superior and inferior positions.[5]

Such units are "orders" in the fact of common association, life style, attitudinal responses and other characteristics of status groups but they are also delineated in economic terms —sources of income, income levels, kinds of occupations. (The term "socio-economic level" is used synonymously.)

What distinguishes the "social class" as a concept from either the Marxist or the Weberian usages is its mix of communal and societal elements. The system of class is clearly distinguished from that of caste through the imputed degree and ease of mobility. "A system of classes, unlike a system of castes, provides *by its own values* [Italics mine—JG] for movement up and down the social ladder."[6]

Warner's finding of a loose structure of continuous gradations has held up remarkably well for the United States and is readily utilizable in European and Japanese countries as well. There is a vast array of associations and correlations between socio-economic level, or social class, and various indices of behavior; even the arenas of political conflict show the same patterns of association. For our purpose here, however, the crucial finding is the amount of overlap; the lack of neat fit between categories of social class and behavior even though the general tendencies are clear. Problems of class values, of worker conservatism, of white-collar radicalism are all part of the imprecision yet utility of the class designations. Differences exist between classes but there is much overlap.

These studies underline the fluidity in the designation of classes as empirical groups; social classes are vague, diffuse and their boundaries are difficult to define. The perceptions of group membership vary both within and between social levels, and an ideology of class exclusiveness is lacking. What is described is less a clearly delineated structure, as in the estates model or the caste model, where boundaries are neatly set, but a system of gradations which flow into each other and between which movement is both possible and does occur.

This characteristic of gradations is discoverable in socialist as well as in capitalist societies. Writing in the early 1950s, the Polish sociologist Stanislaw Ossowski examined contemporary class structure in industrialized societies of both economic forms and pointed to many of their similarities in the fluidity and lack of discrete boundaries of their class structures. He referred to these as modes of "non-egalitarian classlessness."[7]

The inexact character of class and status orders in contemporary industrial societies illustrates the fluid quality of their structures. The mix of class and status in a pattern of gradations of "social class" implies limits to both the division of labor or status designations to describe the division of society into definite groups with the solidarity, mutual obligations and intensity of loyalty characteristically assumed for such communal associations as kin, family, religious fellowship or ethnic community.

Neither can the divisions of society be described as clearly and unambiguously as those of mutual interest based on economic or political interest. The kind of closed and solidary group implied in Weber's view of status is belied by the mixture of class and status elements that cut across each other. The kind of communal development emerging from a common place in the division of labor, described by Marx, is belied by the ways in which life styles and status designations, such as ethnic, religious and educational categories, cut across class lines.

Stratification theory had led sociologists to believe that "primordial" constellations would disappear as industrial evolution produced a more class-like society. They saw com-

F

munal groupings vanishing into classes. The exclusivity and loyalty of status groups was seen as traits of groups at the "closed" end of the scale opposite the "open" form of a class order. They were destined to disappear in the transition from a traditional to a modern social order.

Pluralistic Affiliations

This formulation of social structures is again a mode of dual types. An emphasis on class *or* status, caste or class, closed or open creates a monistic view of society. In this perspective, the participation of the person in the wider society occurs through some single, all-encompassing group like a set of tiers piled one on top of the other. In contrast societies can be seen as composed of a multiplicity of groups, no one of which need be totally absorptive of particular persons and aggregates. For the geological metaphor of rock strata, one on top of another, I would substitute the image of striation: veins of ore running through rock in irregular vertical and horizontal patterns.

My analysis suggests an alternative view of modern and changing societies than that implied in the class or social class positions above. It differs from Weber in that it places less emphasis on the conflict between class and status and greater emphasis on the kind of interrelated roles these often imply. I have indicated the ways in which societal designations, such as class, are blurred in modern society.

In this chapter, the societal *and* class element of communal groups must be emphasized. Society and community can be used as analytical opposites but often they are empirically opposite sides of a coin. Crucial aspects of social change emerge by virtue of their commingling as well as their contrast. Failure to recognize and amplify this has been a major fallacy of stratification theory and of modernization perspectives.

There are some significant differences in the conceptions of how social units relate to each other that are of great importance in understanding stratification. The individual may "belong" to a diversity of organizations and groups and perform a variety of roles in different arenas of his social life. This pluralistic pattern, however, may be unrelated to any one or few defining relationships or may be so closely associated as to make the multiple affiliations and roles an extension of his or her single group membership. A highly societal, rationally motivated organization like the Book of the Month Club, is composed of people who share little more than a general level of education and use of the English language. A joint stock company where stockholders participate in an impersonal, anonymous and highly special form of economic interest is another example. These are truly interracial, interreligious, interethnic associations and thus very attenuated forms of community; almost the quintessence of the societal. For much of social life complete articulation between roles is uncommon. One's job, religion, political status, schooling, forms of medical care are not highly conditioned by any single group affiliation.

A clear exception—the "place" of the American Negro in pre-1970 United States—makes the case more intelligible. For the Negro, the fact of being black has been a matter of central importance in almost every arena of life. A pluralistic society lacks this kind of clustering of roles around one common definition or category.

But the distinction is too forced. In empirical reality roles demonstrate degrees of clustering. There are affinities and associations which *are* associated with each; membership in one implies the other. This is certainly the conclusion of the many social class studies discussed above. Much of the standard sociological research of the past thirty years has underscored the correlations and associations between such attributes and variables as family origin, religion, ethnicity, residence and other social categories and other roles and forms of behavior, including political vote, occupational choice, life chances, fertility and the myriad minutiae of institutional study.

In an effort to understand conflict and its emergence or

dormancy, Ralf Dahrendorf has suggested that these differences in forms and degrees of clustering are an important
clue to the rise of conflict.

> When conflict groups encounter each other in several
> associations and in several clashes, the energies expended
> in all of them will be combined and one overriding conflict
> of interests will emerge. . . . If, on the other hand, the in-
> evitable pluralism of associations is accompanied by a
> pluralism of fronts of conflict, none of these is likely to
> develop the intensity of class conflicts of the Marxian
> type.[8]

In the history of political conflict in the United States, the
intensity of moral issues, such as alcohol, abortion, Sunday
laws and other non-economic concerns were heightened by
the fact that they posed oppositions between people who
were at the same time chiefly Protestant, rural, middle-class,
native American against people who were at the same time
Catholic, urban, working class and immigrant. A number of
attributes clustered together. In contemporary America such
clustering on the basis of Catholic and Protestant has been
lessened, although it has by no means disappeared.

These two forms of pluralism have very different consequences and must be distinguished. In one, several distinct
groups—societal, communal and mixed—cohere in a single
area of social life. This is the "pluralism of fronts" that I refer
to as *linked pluralities* since various separate social units are
linked in an association. The prior and external identities are
blurred and minimized in *this* relationship for this purpose.
The joint association of White, Catholic, Protestant and
Jewish clergy in the American civil rights movement of the
1960s is an instance of linked pluralism. In the other form of
pluralism where attributes of a communal identity cluster
into another area, such as an aspect of the division of labor,
we will refer to *segmented pluralities*. Here the coming
together of members of the same community in roles and
activities creates an entire social area—a segment of the total

society. The coherence and centrality of the Catholic in the Ulster lower class is one such form of segmentation today.

Social Segmentation

To use a chemical analogy: in a pattern of segmented pluralities diverse social groups are precipitated out at different levels of the social test tube. Points in the social structure—territory, occupation, institution and class—are heavily represented by particular and self-conscious social groups—lineage, race, ethnic, caste, religious and cultural. Innumerable examples of such segmentation can be cited. In Timbuctoo, before the French conquest, there was a guild system of hereditary crafts which assured that occupation and lineage coincided: slipper makers were Arma; tailors were Alfi; smiths were Songhai. Studies of a New England shoe factory in the 1940s found a system of ethnic stratification in the work levels: unskilled workers were French-Canadian; foremen and supervisors were Irish-American; the executive posts were held by native American Yankee New Englanders. The virtual exclusivity of these lines were maintained by informal sponsorship and, in crisis, by strikes and protests. The conflicts between Hindu and Muslim in India during the twentieth century have been accentuated because, as in Ulster, the religious differences also coincide with those of economic class.

The sources and sequences of such segmentation are manifold. The time of entry of migrating groups into a society; the skills already distributed and their relation to structural opportunities; the myths and beliefs of social groups about each other—all contribute to the clustering of communal groups into particular segmented areas of social institutions and hierarchical levels. Since cultures and power are seldom distributed randomly at any point in history, roles and positions often follow group lines. The transmission of capital, skill and sponsorship within lineage, religious and other communal boundaries perpetuates and supports the segmentation once it emerges. Even in the American underworld, entry into effective organizations is greatly aided by membership in the "right" ethnic communities.

Prevailing sociological theory has ignored these considerations and has viewed industrialism, urbanism and bureaucratic organizations as great solvents of communal hierarchies and as catalysts of class division. Yet the processes of industrialization and the division of labor have not served to eradicate communal identities in the economic or work arenas. Everett Hughes has pointed out how such rationalistic processes, ostensibly the embodiments of disinterested, unsentimental forces devoid of group ties and appeals, have actually often resulted in specialization and stratification by communal memberships:

> ... modern industry, by virtue of being the great mixer, has inevitably been a colossal agent of racial, religious and ethnic segregation. ... Industry brings people together and sorts them out for various kinds of work; the sorting will, where the mixture is new, of necessity follow the racial and ethnic lines. For cultures ... differ in nothing more than in the skills, work habits and goals which they instill into the individual ... industry is almost universally an agent of racial and ethnic discrimination. ... For those who hire industrial help must nearly always choose from among people who are not all alike ethnically, and very often from among ethnic groups whose industrial training and experience are far from equal.[9]

In both kinds of process, linked pluralities and social segmentation, the conflict between community and society, tradition and modernity is neither necessary nor anticipated. In each case, the potential exists in theory for the coherence and even reinforcement of one process by another. The existent situation cannot be anticipated on the basis of a theory of social evolution. In each case, the historical character of the situation and society involved and the precise area of social life in question are highly significant. A linear view of change is inconsistent with these realities.

Class, Community and Reductionism

Those who see communal ties as insignificant in modern society may use this discussion as proof of their contention that societal elements, especially those of economic class, are dominant in contemporary societies. By this reasoning, the bonds of communal membership are reducible to class interest in maintaining or changing the allocation of resources. The fact that ethnic, racial, religious or other communal groups can be described as occupying structural positions is interpreted in such a way that their communal identities are unimportant to an understanding of their political behavior or conflicts with other groups.

Such reductions are fallacious. They ignore the intensity aroused by definition of social conflicts in communal terms rather than as interests flowing from structural positions. The alliances of communities that cut across class boundaries and flow from communal imagery are too salient to be ignored. The 1946–7 Hindu-Muslim conflicts in India may have emerged in a context of class struggle between peasant and landlord, worker and employer. They were neither construed nor directed in such a manner that class ties were emphasized. Nor were Hindus and Muslims allied when they represented the same economic position. The emergence of anti-semitism among some Black spokesmen in New York City in the late 1960s illustrates the point. The issues of schools and teachers pitted the Black parents against the school teachers, a large percentage of whom were Jewish. While there were economic interests, and participants were conscious of them, the conflict was also seen as one of communities, strongly accentuating the depth of Jewish and Black resentments and by no means creating a unity among all the school teachers. Because communities are also interest groups, the mix of class and community, of the societal and the communal, is not readily reduced to one or the other part of the dichotomy without great loss in understanding. Glazer and Moynihan's statement about New York City is equally true for many other societies:

> ... all policies in the city *are* inevitably policies for race and ethnic relations. This is inevitable because the ethnic and racial groups of the city are also interest groups, based on jobs and occupations and possessions. Nor are they interest groups alone; they are also attached to symbols of their past, they are concerned with the fate of their homelands, they want to see members of their group raised to high position and respect.[10]

Communal Organization, Stratification Theory and National Development

The interactive character of much communal and societal organization, their blending of both class and caste-like characteristics, provides great difficulty for the individualistic imagery of much modernization theory. Granted that there are economic interests which divide the population, the relation of these to communal bonds of both obligation and opportunity are of central importance to the mobilization of conflict and to further maintenance and change within the system of stratification. *The "mix" of the two communal and societal types is of more importance than their differences.* This realization is crucial to the analysis of nation-building in the newly independent nations.

The significance of cultural, ethnic and racial segmentation was apparent to Western social scientists and administrators who observed the colonial patterns of Asia in the late nineteenth and early twentieth centuries. In the concepts of "dual societies" and "plural societies," J. H. Boeke and J. S. Furnivall separately described "societies" in which social segmentation was deep and divisive.

For Boeke, writing about Indonesia, in *The Evolution of the Netherlands Indies Economy,* Western capitalism had been imported into a precapitalistic agrarian economy which the Indonesians resisted in practice. The result was a dual economy; an urban capitalistic one in which Chinese, Europeans and Indonesians traded in a market economy and a village economy which operated by different principles, more attuned to demands of custom and the struggle for prestige than to material advantage.

Furnivall's usage, much closer to our problems, emphasized the cleavage of distinct groups—ethnic, racial or caste —and the weak solidarity between them. The "plural society" Furnivall described in *Colonial Policy and Practice* was not so much separated by diverse economic logics as by communal sentiments of in-group cohesion and out-group hostility: It is "...a society... comprising two or more elements or orders which live side by side, yet without mingling in one *political* unit."[11]

In his descriptions, especially those of Indonesia and Burma, Furnivall pictured a society with deep social segmentation along ethnic lines. The Indonesian occupied the lower, more menial and less prestigious jobs; the Chinese played a customary middleman role in retail and wholesale trade between the Europeans and the Indonesians. Such societies, however, are not to be likened or analogized to the agrarian, feudal societies of traditional sociological theory. The alleged unity of obligations and dependencies between strata is lacking in Furnivall's plural societies. Neither are they encompassed in the pluralistic political systems of the West, as I have discussed those above.

For Furnivall, *community* in Asia is *communalism*—a system of conflict in which each community recognizes only its betterment as legitimate. It gives an anomic, predatory character to relations between groups, unmediated by a sense of membership in any common social unit. When people meet in the marketplace, on societal grounds, the result is cut-throat behavior unchecked by a consensus about social ends:

In a homogeneous society the soldier looks at social problems from the standpoint of the soldier, the merchant ... as a merchant and the cultivator as a cultivator; yet at the same time they regard such problems from the standpoint of a *common citizenship.* [They] cannot wholly disregard the views and interests of other classes. ... there is a conflict of interest ... but the asperity of conflict is softened by a common citizenship [pp. 451–2, italics mine—JG].

The Hobbesian world of J. S. Furnivall is the nightmare of those who see communal loyalties as threatening to engulf and destroy both new nations and old ones as they search for national unity amid the cultures and diversities of the past. The "closed" or "open" character of the economy may have very different implications for social and political conflict depending on whether or not the mobility achievable diminishes or increases the social segmentation of communal groups.

The contradictions between traditional sociological theories of stratification and the description of plural societies might be attributed to the impact of colonial rule. With the development of independence and "modern" economic development, it might be expected that communal groups would be greatly weakened and class structures emerge. I have already shed some dissenting light on this in discussing castes in India in an earlier chapter. Here the point is made again from another standpoint. "Modern" forces are by no means inimical to communal groups; they even support and reinforce their emergence and importance in political and economic life. In India, caste groups have been undergoing a process of transformation from localistic associations to regional and even national groups. Education, increased areas of communication and transportation, physical mobility and even occupational mobility enhance the cohesion and widened scope of castes, religions and linguistic groups in India. Furnivall saw similar processes in Indonesia. As the Chinese developed wealth the increased education did not lead to merger into a "westernized" class of Indonesian elites.

Instead they hired mainland Chinese to set up schools, and they taught Chinese and imported newspapers which increased their separateness and enhanced their self-conception of difference. Mobility did not imply the dissolution of communal sentiments.

Maurice Freedman has made the same point for Malaya, noting the ways in which a nationalized politics had brought about a broader conception of the ethnic groups in Malayan politics:

> Malay was and remains a culturally plural society . . . its plural character is more marked today than ever before. Nationalism and political independence in their early phases have tended to define, on a pan-Malayan basis, ethnic blocs which in former times were merely categories. Then the social map of Malay was . . . made up of a kaleidoscope of small culturally defined units. . . . "The Malays" did not interact with "the Chinese" and "the Indians". . . . But as "Malays," "Chinese" and "Indians" come to be realized as structural entities on a nation-wide scale, they can begin to have total relations with one another.[12]

This should not be taken as a denial of the development of class characteristics and organization in new nations. As Beteille indicated above, class relationships and class formations *are* emerging in India, in an individualistic manner. So, too, the political role of castes in new electoral politics produces class interests both as uniting forces and as elements of internal conflict. Beteille's own qualifications to his emphasis on emergent class organization in India can equally be used to qualify the opposite emphasis on the continuity of castes:

> But it has to be clearly realized that if caste has to be rejected as the total social structure, it cannot be replaced by *class* as some might wish. I have often heard the argument that caste conflicts are really distorted expressions of

more fundamental social conflicts—in short, class conflicts. . . . They have to be rejected on the same grounds as those for rejecting caste as *the* total or basic social structure. No such thing exists in reality. . .[13]

Looked at from still another vantage point, the dichotomy of community and society underlying the caste-class distinction has prevented another aspect of stratification from receiving adequate recognition. It has led to a failure to perceive the importance of group affiliations and actions in the achievement of economic and social mobility. The phenomenon of social segmentation underscores the importance of informal, social bonds in making various opportunity structures available. Communal membership often reinforces utilitarian, societal functions. Patterns of cooperative pooling of resources for capital loans, for example, have enabled some ethnic groups to utilize their communal sources of trust and obligation to aid entrepreneurial activity. Light's study of the Chinese, Japanese and West Indians in the United States has shown that even with the absence of banking facilities, these "traditional" means of capital development were crucial bases of mobility. Extended family ties enabled these immigrants to utilize small amounts from several kin to form enough capital to originate businesses.

There is still another aspect of group mobility, however, which an individuated, class-oriented view of stratification tends to miss: mobility through group or community politics. I have already indicated how social segmentation makes so much of public policy significant for communal groups. It is also the case that communal groups utilize their cohesive qualities for the purposes of influencing the status and class interests of members. The role of ethnicity, race and religion in American politics is a salient example of how politics has been used to affect the interests of communities. Gaining status through appointments is one well-recognized route to increased communal status. However, there are communal aspects to many issues which are seemingly unrelated to cultural diversities. Even issues of local governmental forms can be the cause of communal conflicts and loyalties. The conflict between city manager and mayoral forms of municipal government in the United States, for example, has often been implicated in the opportunities for jobs. The greater professionalism of the city manager government has operated to the detriment of lower income groups, whose access to city jobs rested on the informal, non-professionalized sponsorship of urban machine politics. Commenting on the general pattern of city manager–mayor conflicts, Meyerson and Banfield remark that almost everywhere in the United States the lower classes oppose the council-manager form while the upper classes support it. Reporting a study of Jackson, Michigan which they say throws light on the motives involved and on the mix of class and religion. "The first thing that the council did. . . It discharged most of the Catholics and replaced them mostly by Protestants . . . the new council celebrated the establishment of the new form of government with a reception in the Masonic Temple."[14]

It is not only in the United States that the political arena is the scene of communal efforts toward mobility. In the context of Indian political democracy, caste struggles have neither diminished nor been replaced by class conflicts. Caste communities persist and find new expression through the election campaign and the ballot box. Castes, operating through associations or political parties, find national and state politics an effective channel for achieving better allocation of resources, recognition of status through caste candidates and even legitimation of caste mobility through name changes. Among accounts of caste politics is the case of the Palli, a humble agricultural caste of Madras State. Their century-old effort to gain recognition as Vanniyars, a much higher caste of Kshatriyas, culminated in the post-Independence period when they were able to use their electoral strength as a lever in mobility aims and get other, more powerful castes to grant recognition to their new status.

What is central to our analysis of this use of modernizing changes is not the fact that castes, ethnic groups or other communal associations continue to persist, albeit in changed

forms. Theories of transitional arrangements are consistent
with this. Such theories posit a transitional stage between
the traditional and the modern in which the two types are
commingled. What is asserted here however is that the very
aspects of linear theories which are posited as sources
weakening the communal units, in many cases emerge as
reinforcements for them. Lynch, describing this process in
the political mobilization of Untouchables in Agra (India)
expresses this idea well. Referring to a change from efforts to
imitate Sanskritic (Brahmin) customs, in the strategies of the
Jatavs, an Untouchable "caste," Lynch wrote:

> . . . Sanskritization is no longer as effective a means as is
> political party participation for achieving a change in style
> of life and a rise in the Indian social system, now composed
> of both caste and class elements.[15]

Caste, as a principle of social organization, is undergoing
much change but its usage as a focus of communal bonds
remains and is even intensified by the political impact of
democratic, egalitarian and electoral competition. Old caste
struggles continue in new arenas; new caste associations
pursue new objectives. To a significant extent, the equali-
tarian character of politics after Independence has meant
both a recomposition and a growing equality of castes rather
than their disappearance and substitution by emerging class
structure.

Nation, Citizenship and Community

This same mixture of types is evident when we consider the
implications and processes of national development and
nationhood in the light both of stratification theories and the
linear account of social change. Against the presumed
tendencies of egalitarian institutions to emphasize and
develop class and societal groups, nationalist sentiment and
nationalistic movements appear to be contradictions. Both

Marxist and non-Marxist sociologists have had difficulty in reconciling the success of appeals to national solidarity with theories of class or other interest aims as determinative of political behavior and conflict.

Stratification theory and the "community-society" dichotomy have heavily influenced the theories of nation-building which have been current in the study of social change. These have assumed that ascribed criteria of membership and recruitment and closed systems of social mobility are inherently inimical to the development of modern political organization. According to many observers of new nations, the view is held that kinship, locality, religion, caste and the panoply of primordial ties act as deterrents to the emergence of national bonds of loyalty and dedication in the newly independent countries of Asia and Africa.

> Almost everywhere the societies consist of relatively discrete collectives—ethnic, *communal* [Italic ours—JG], caste, religious or linguistic—that have little sense of identity with one another or with the national whole.[16]

The growth and stability of the nation-state are thus seen as necessitating the dissolution of closed social units and the incorporation of people into larger, more open national and class groups, bound together by ties of national sentiment and interests of utilitarian purpose. In similar fashion, Max Weber argued that Christianity had been an important source for the development of urban political association. As a universal religion, it diminished the importance of local, communal differences in the larger status of common Christian fellowship. Other primordial affiliations conflicted less with the common membership of everyone in the urban territory as Christians. The idea of the citizenship of all Christians was thus possible in the face of otherwise contradictory diversities.

In this section, two major points are asserted: (1) the ideas of citizenship and egalitarian political forms, while creating opportunities for the development of class structure, have also been significant in the development of cohesion, solidarity and a sense of political community on a widened base of national sentiments and structures. (2) While, under some conditions, communal identities have been impediments to nation-building, under other conditions they have been important sources of national identity.

The ambivalence and critical stance which nineteenth-century intellectuals had toward the idea of equality has been continued in the analysis of nationalism. The wars of Europe, the rise of Hitler and the doctrine of the Herrenvolk, the belief that Russian foreign policy is as nationalistic as other Western countries, have all given rise to a skepticism concerning the possibility that class and interest ties will emerge to dominate and modify the intensity of the sentiments of national feeling.

Two sociologists as diverse in perspective and philosophy as Reinhard Bendix and Hannah Arendt provide us with an underlying common assessment of the potentialities of egalitarian political structure for national sentiments. In his study *Nation-Building and Citizenship*, Bendix examined the transition from a master-servant relationship between political elites and the lower orders to one of political equality through the spread of citizenship. Building on studies of seventeenth- and eighteenth-century protest movements, he advanced the thesis that by the late eighteenth and early nineteenth century in France and England, the protests of lower classes were actuated *both* by economic interests and by aspirations toward political and social equality. The granting of citizenship was essential to the industrializing societies as a means to quell organized protest and to assure the necessary cooperation of the lower classes in the industrialization of the society. This process of drawing all social segments into the political community has continued with the rise of Welfare State attitudes and the effective participation of a more educated, powerful and self-conscious electorate.

While new nations face many different problems and situations, they do find the creation of a political community through a more participative electorate to be a necessity for economic development. Whether we refer to a totalitarian, pluralist or some other version of political structure, the idea of a national community, a political "people" is fed both by economic demands for a wider economic market and a cooperative work force and by the ideological strains accompanying the diffusion of ideas and the struggles for independence.

Arendt's study, *The Origins of Totalitarianism*, is much more specific and particular: it is an attempt to account for the rise of totalitarianism in Europe. She saw the decay of class structure and the nation-state as culminating in a mass society which produced the malaise of the twentieth-century political movements of Europe. Like Bendix, she also sees in the development of citizenship a basic conception of equality and national participation. Emphasizing the potential solidarity and/or "tyranny" of majorities, she described ways in which popular sentiments minimize and adjure distinctions and differences.

> The more equal conditions, the less explanation there is for the differences that actually exist between people and thus all the more unequal do individuals and groups become.[17]

Arendt located the source of the totalitarian movements in those groups that were politically indifferent and unincorporated into German and Russian political life. The sudden eruption of these masses into political consciousness was the trigger of European revolutionary history in the twentieth century:

> ...democratic government had rested as much on the silent approbation and tolerance of the indifferent and inarticulate sections of the people as on the articulate and visible institutions and organizations of the country.[18]

In these perspectives there is a strong recognition that the emergence of societal associations and citizenship is not

G

inimical to nation-building. Rather, it is a positive buttress to using the nation as the focal symbol of communal sentiments. Whatever may be the fate of local territory, the modern period is by no means a destroyer of the idea or reality of the mix of territory and "peoplehood."

The second point is a further recognition of the complex mix of types in the reality of events. While communal differences are a clear source of impediment to nation-building, they may also, and often, be a means by which individuals are more clearly able to form a relationship with the larger community of the nation. The quotation from Maurice Freedman about Malaysia above has already made the point that a national, participative politics has widened the scope and definition of ethnic and regional groups. In seeking rewards and resources on a national level, the primordial community is made a part of the national sphere, both in its segmented, economic aspects, and in its status in a national system of stratification. Jobs, prestige, education are all part of the commitments to institutions and arrangements beyond the level of the pre-existent community. They mitigate and modify the impediments otherwise imposed by the cultural diversities of primordial communities.

Neither has the nationalism of new nations meant the disappearance of cultural or communal diversities. Neither national homogeneity nor processes of individuation have destroyed the local and cultural distinctions of many societies. Whereas in a number of instances—such as the Hindu–Muslim conflicts, the tribal antagonisms of Nigeria or the religious animosities of North Ireland—these have been incompatible with national sentiments and loyalties, in others they have been a source of support. Both Untouchables and many middle-level castes in India have used traditional structures of social differentiation as primary political mechanisms of mobilization for electoral strength. They have found a modern commitment to national India in the group equality implicit in a participative political system. American ethnic groups have not been diluted in the crucible of the melting pot but that very cohesion has been a means through which their aspirations for mobility and autonomy have strengthened nationalist ties.

To sum up, the egalitarianism implicit in national emergence does not appear to be inherently inconsistent with stratification based on communal and caste characteristics. Indeed, participative politics grants communities considerable recognition and support.

Lastly, nationalism is itself a new form of communal identity. The soldiers of the French Revolution represented the first citizen army in the history of Europe; an army which could depend on a sense of common man toward "King and Country." As a polity dependent on a sense of common identity of its citizens as one "people," the nation is a product of the modern period. Whatever its debt to industrial development, to egalitarian ideas or to capitalistic institutions, it is one of the most prevalent and intense forms of communal grouping in the contemporary world.

Conclusion: The Fallacies of Modernization Theory

In this chapter I have considered sociological theories of stratification as they have affected the study of social change. The dichotomy between "community and society" has played a significant role in the development of such theories, especially in the distinction between "tradition and modernity." Nevertheless, the results of a variety of studies of new nations and of Western societies indicates the insufficiency of the theories and the version of social change underlying them.

The crux of the difficulty is the mixed character of the concepts as referents to the real world. It is not, as some have suggested, that the concepts are "ideal types" and the empirical reality locatable at some point on a continuum between the two. More significantly, the processes supposed to weaken communal systems of stratification do not do so; in fact, they are just as likely to strengthen them; to support both communal and societal groups; or to appear in conflict.

In the analysis of specific and concrete events, the concepts become blurred and their coexistence and mutual interaction more important than their clash and conflict.

The linear theory of evolutionary change perceived social change as moving away from one set of conditions and toward another: from community to society. The coherence of both forms and the problematic relation between them in specific, empirical cases makes the theory unacceptable as a scientific description of how social change occurs or is occurring today. In positing "community" as opposite "society," "tradition" opposite "modernity," both the evolutionary sociologists and the modernization theorists have given an overly simplified and distorted picture of how and in what direction change takes place in contemporary life.

Notes to Chapter 3

[1] Wilbert Moore, *Social Change*, Englewood Cliffs, Prentice-Hall, 1963; pp. 89–90.

[2] André Beteille, *Castes: Old and New*, New Delhi, 1969; p. 58.

[3] Karl Marx, *The Poverty of Philosophy*, quoted in Nicolai Bukharin, *Historical Materialism*, New York, 1925; p. 293.

[4] Max Weber, *From Max Weber*, trans. and edited by Hans Gerth and C. Wright Mills, New York and London, 1946; p. 183.

[5] W. Lloyd Warner and Paul Lunt, *The Social Life of a Modern Community*; p. 82.

[6] See note 5.

[7] Stanislaw Ossowski, *Class Structure in the Social Consciousness*, London, 1963; esp. pp. 100–21.

[8] Ralf Dahrendorf, *Class and Class Conflict in Industrial Society*, Palo Alto, California and London, 1959; p. 215.

[9] Everett C. Hughes, *When Peoples Meet*, Glencoe, Illinois, 1952; pp. 64–5.

[10] Glazer and Moynihan, op. cit., second edition, 1970; p. lxxxiii.

[11] J. H. Furnivall, Colonial *Policy and Practice*, p. 446.

[12] Maurice Freedman, "The Growth of a Plural Society in Malaya" *Pacific Affairs* 33; (1960), 158–67. Quoted in Geertz, op. cit., p. 154.

[13] André Beteille, "Closed and Open Social Stratification in India" in Beteille, op. cit., p. 86.

[14] Martin Meyerson and Edward Banfield, *Politics, Planning and the Public Interest*, Glencoe, Illinois, 1955; p. 290.

[15] Owen Lynch, *The Politics of Untouchability*, New York, 1969; p. 97.

[16] Edward Shils, "On the Comparative Study of the New States" in Geertz, op. cit., p. 3.

[17] Hannah Arendt, *The Origins of Totalitarianism*, New York and London, 1951; p. 54.

[18] Ibid., p. 306.

4

THE SEARCH FOR COMMUNITY
Concepts as Utopias

Semantic and Poetic Meanings

There is an apocryphal tale about a sociologist who was noted for the depth of his scientific and skeptical analysis. It was said of him that he spent the first twelve weeks of a thirteen week term tearing down the religious faiths and moral certainties with which the freshman entered college. He demonstrated the natural source of religious beliefs the student had accepted as revealed truth. He pointed to the customs and rituals of primitive tribes and other societies to show the relative and conventional character of moralities. In the thirteenth week, however, he provided a "higher synthesis" which restored the faith and morals of the student but on a new and more sophisticated base. One year he was called out of town for the final week and the campus has never been the same since.

Like the sociologist in my story, I propose to restore the concept of "community," and its corollary, "society" to the good graces of scholars, intellectuals and other students. And, like the story above, I propose to do so by placing it on another basis; by demonstrating that it is more than one kind of concept. Having belabored the difficulties of using these concepts as scientific terms to describe and analyze types of human associations, I now want to consider them as something other than scientific concepts. Having criticized the theory of social change implicit in the dichotomy, I now want to place that theory in a context of activity rather than analysis.

Concepts embody generalizations. Certainly "community and society" express both a belief in the incompatibility between forms of human association and a theory of social change. Such generalizations are not the embodiment of experiment and experience but are, instead, the perspectives which are used to make that experience possible. They provide a means to order and interpret that experience as lying along a particular line, having a particular significance and leading to particular advice. They do so at the cost, as in the case of the communal-society dualism, of distorting the complexity of human behavior to a point which becomes misleading as descriptive and predictive instruments; as scientific terms.

However, there is another side to human concepts. Peter Winch has expressed this aptly in writing: "To give an account of the meaning of a word is to describe how it is used and to describe how it is used is to describe the social intercourse into which it enters."[1] That use is not only as an instrument by scholars to represent and analyze the world as it is. Concepts also serve in a context in which men and women are assessing, choosing and committing themselves to actions and attitudes. We have already seen this process at work in our analysis of Durkheim and the nineteenth-century theorists in Chapter 1 where we looked at concepts as embodying ideologies. It is that use which I will probe more closely as it occurs in contemporary life and as it elucidates meanings and uses of concepts at other than levels of empirical analysis and description.

Literary critics and philosophers have given much thought to the differences between scientific and non-scientific language. One literary critic, Kenneth Burke, provides us with a useful distinction between *semantic* and *poetic* meanings of words and terms. Semantic meanings have a true or false character to them. They designate something in such a fashion that everyone can utilize it in the same way. They have a neutral cast. "Community" as a term to describe a form of human association which exists, is representative of a reality; has asemantic meaning. The assertions of that meaning can be true or false. Poetic meaning involves a perspective which constitutes what is significant from one or another perspective; it takes an attitude toward an object or event. Semantic meanings strive for clarity and the eradication of emotive meaning; poetic meaning strives for inclusion of a moral perspective.

[The semantic meaning] fosters ... the notion that one may comprehensively discuss human and social events in a non-moral vocabulary ... It is the moral impulse that motivates perception giving it both intensity and direction, suggesting *what to look for* and *what to look out for*. Only by wanting very profoundly to make improvement, can we get a glimpse into the devious personal and impersonal factors that balk improvement.[2]

From this standpoint, our contrasting concepts have to be seen as poetic as well as semantic. They represent those aspects and points in contemporary life which have significance and relevance for people who seek answers to the question: what shall we aim toward in our social relationships? in the development of our society? Community becomes an idealized, invented depiction of a social organization which is to be approached or drawn away from. As such, it is not inconsistent with a scientific or semantic meaning but it possesses another meaning above and around its literal scientific one.

The realization of concepts as imbued with poetic qualities provides us with appreciation of the metaphorical and mythic side of the community-society contrast. In metaphor we connect qualities of one object with a seemingly different object, as in "a balloon face" to describe a child. Community and society are metaphorical in that they are linked up to certain typical experiences which provide for the reader a means of identifying what the author intends. Thus the communal relationship is epitomized in the *warmth* of the family; the societal in the *coldness* of the rational contract. The communal stratification is *closed*; the societal is *open*. The descriptive words (warm-cold; closed-open) provide a moral significance. In using the family or the contract as typical situations the concepts take those situations as metaphors to equate to themselves.

The terms of contrast are also mythic. Myth is neither true nor false but presents a belief in a past or future situation or event on which the present action can be based. The myth of the founding fathers of the United States constitution is a source of the legitimacy of that document; referred to as a basis for a framework of law outside the discretionary whims or wisdoms of living judges. Whether "community" has ever come close to the ideal form which the conceptual term and the theory indicate, belief in that existence provides a backdrop for judging contemporary life and generates an "ideal" for the future.

Lastly, the concepts of community and society, in their poetic meanings, do for human activity what scientific concepts cannot do: they provide drama and conflict, without which choices are pointless. Throughout this essay I have emphasized the imputed conflict and clash between communal and societal forms of association. Much of the first three chapters has been devoted to refuting this conflict as a scientific finding. Viewed as drama, as protagonist and antagonist, the terms of the conceptual dualism are less about scientific description, analysis and prediction than they are about the kind of future toward which we, as active human beings, *should* aim. They are less about the Past than about the evaluation of the Present.

It is in this sense that I want to examine the use of these concepts as *utopias*—as visions of the future and the present about which men and women are arguing. The pursuit of scientific knowledge is a way, perhaps the characteristic idiom of the modern age, through which this discussion is conducted. "Community and society" are not only concepts of social analysis. "Modernity" is not just a term of science.

These are also goals toward which people move or from which they are repelled.

These images of past and of future owe much of their content to perspectives and evaluations toward the present. As diagnoses and prescriptions for present ills, they operate as Utopian ideals, organizing a contrast to the present and providing a direction toward the future. In this fashion, the concept shifts, changes and takes on new meanings and connotations.

The discussion of "community and society" which occupied the attention of the nineteenth- and early twentieth-century writers has continued to dominate much of the analysis and evaluation of contemporary intellectuals as well. The context of the discussion has changed. The active pursuit of change among new nations in Asia and Africa has raised again the question of the value of industrial development, technological change and egalitarian social institutions in contrast to the usages identified with the presumed communal life of the past. In the industrialized nations, there is no longer an argument about whether or not the changes leading to greater technological specialization, urbanization and a wider equality should occur. They are by now accomplished facts and the question is rather how we should respond to what is by now "the nature of things." These responses, at once political and intellectual, are the focus of this chapter.

The Little Community: The Utopia of the Past

One of the prevalent images of contemporary social science is of the small town, the village, the farm settlement as the embodiment of lost virtues. In the process of urbanization and centralization, the decline of the rural and small community is one of the major stories of sociology. As a character in this plot, the little community appears in a leading role.

This need to recreate the past as an ideal of human relationships is one *leit-motif* of the current intellectual age.

As one example, here is Fritz Pappenheim's depiction of Marx's views on industrial growth and the alienation of the worker:

> The social framework of modern industrialized nations described by Marx is in many ways the archetype of Toennie's Gesellschaft . . . (Marx describes) the structure of a social order in which the strong communal organization of previous societies—for example, of tribal communities or medieval towns—no longer exists. In such societies individuals have become so separated and isolated that they establish contact *only* (Italics mine. JG) when they can use each other as means to particular ends; bonds between human beings are supplanted by useful associations; not of whole persons but of particularized individuals.[3]

In so viewing the development of society out of the destruction of community, such writers evoke the theme of alienation from human relationships that is so redolent in modern thought. The estrangement and isolation of modern man from his fellow human beings and social institutions is seen not as the human condition but as a falling away, a consequence of the movement from past to present. In this shape, the typology of community and society is not only an empirical usage, it is also a mythical device which expresses a present emotion.

In American and British life the myth of the little community has appeared in the glorification of the qualities of small-town and rural farm life and the accompanying condemnation of the city as the source of evil. The "myth of the yeoman," as Richard Hofstadter has referred to it,[4] has shaped a significant part of political belief and action. The imputed self-sufficiency, independence, honesty, and direct relation to nature of the farmer are in sharp contrast to the deviousness, artificiality and complex quality of life in the cities. The farmer was the ideal citizen and his moral worth was something for government to defend and maintain. The myth was, and still is, a powerful force in shoring up the economic and political interests of agrarian people in their conflicts with an urban economy and city politics.

In the imagery of city-country conflict, the urban centers are described as inhumane, depersonalizing and lacking in just those qualities of common sentiment which the community-society typology has posited. American community studies have discovered ample resonance of this in the talk of small town people about themselves and the city and in many urbanites as well. Vidich and Bensman's study of Springdale, a small town in upstate New York, is one good example of this imagery. In *Small Town in Mass Society*, the inhabitants present a view of the small town as morally superior to the city; a place where people are friendly, neighborly and "just folks" in contrast to the big cities where people are corrupt, selfish and unconcerned about each other.

> Almost all of rural life receives its justification on the basis of the direct and personal and human feelings that guide people's relations with each other.... It is as if the people in a deeply felt communion bring themselves together for the purposes of mutual self-help and protection.[5]

This vision of the lost world of Gemeinschaft certainly was a major theme in much of urbanism theory among sociologists, especially until the mid-1950s. Durkheim's *Division of Labor* had laid the basis for the view of urban societies as destructive of human cohesion based on personal sentiment and common identities. Many of the empirical studies of the University of Chicago School of Sociology during the 1920s and 1930s reiterated the theme sounded in Harvey Zorbaugh's study of *The Gold Coast and the Slum* of the decline and disappearance of community in the modern world. In an autobiographical account, a woman living in the area of furnished rooms, quoted by Zorbaugh, makes the observation:

> ... not a human touch in it all.
> The city is like that. In all my work there had been the

same lack of any personal touch. In all this city of three million souls, I knew no one, was cared for by no one.[6]

The Myth of the Lost Paradise

Whether in the form of a glorification of the past virtues of the little community or in the condemnation of urbanism as the destructive consequence of an *anomic* society, one stream within social theory has accentuated and maintained the myth of a lost paradise, a gemeinschaftliche Utopia which we have lost in creating a world of rational organization, economic exchange and specialized functions. The dichotomy of "community and society" is accepted, to the decided derogation of Society.

In a similar vein, these issues of social evolution have been a persistent focus of debate and conflict in new nations. The value of the village inherent in its customs and social structure has become a salient factor in public policy as many new nations debate the direction that economic development should take. The argument over "tradition" versus "modernity" has often led to the same tendency to describe the village in glowing terms as a repository of the human, the personal and the friendly in contrast to the immoral, secular and *anomic* qualities which modernization brings in its wake. In India, such glorification of the village has been deeply implicit and explicit in Gandhi's efforts to locate economic development in the village and in ways which would not threaten the continuance of the traditional village. The spinning wheel and *khadi* (textile product of domestic, village industry) are symbols of this suspicion and hostility to modernizing. The same apotheosis of the little community has continued among Neo-Ghandians, such as Vinoba Bhave and J. P. Narayan.

The myth of the lost paradise has by no means been accepted by all who have shared its terms of social evolution from community to society. Whether in the nineteenth or the twentieth century, the early Durkheim's more positive appraisal of the modern has been shared. For Marx, ending "the idiocy of rural life" was a positive achievement of capitalism, just as breaking up "the cake of custom" was a valued consequence of social change for the British writer, Walter Bagehot. The sophistication, rationality and tolerance of the urban world were also positive accomplishments of Gesellschaft for the Chicago school of Robert Park and Louis Wirth. These sociologists shared the Utopian description of the past as Gemeinschaft but they saw its disappearance as a blessing rather than a curse. While they saw many problems arising from the decline of the little community, they also saw many assets. Robert Park expressed this in a consistent Durkheimian perspective, emphasizing the narrowness and restrictive tyranny of Gemeinschaft.

> In the freedom of the city every individual, no matter how eccentric, finds somewhere an environment in which he can expand and bring what is peculiar in his nature to some sort of expression. A smaller community sometimes tolerates eccentricity, but the city often rewards it. Certainly one of the attractions of a city is that somewhere every type of individual . . . may find congenial company and the vice or talent which was suppressed in the more intimate circle of the family or in the narrow limits of a small community, discovers here a moral climate in which it flourishes.[7]

The Utopian view of the little community of the past has the quality of myth in two respects. First, it is an image of past reality which organizes attitudes and activities in the present. As a point of reference, it enables the believer to evaluate change. Secondly, as a statement of what has happened in history, its status as fact is ambiguous and incorrect. This latter point is one that needs amplification here.

The character of the dialogue arising through the evolutionary theory of community and society has been a gross oversimplification of the flux and complexity of realities.

Continuously throughout this essay I have pointed to the fallacy of seeing typologies in a zero-sum fashion: The more of community, the less of society and vice-versa. In utilizing one part of the typology as a contrast to the present, the users distort and falsify the situation as it appears to scholars. As Louis Wirth has written in discussing this same dichotomy:

> For purposes of getting an answer to some questions, it is best to conceive of a social group as a community, for others, as a society. They are not two different kinds of group life but two aspects of all human group life.[8]

That Gemeinschaft continues to exist in the context of urban life has been a major conclusion of a wide variety of urban research during the past two decades. Both in industrial and in industrializing societies, the "acids of modernity" have by no means destroyed ethnic ties or kinship loyalties or eradicated the importance of informal, personal relationships. Much of this research has been discussed in earlier chapters, but it is necessary to reiterate it in this context. Studies of cities as seemingly disparate as Tokoyo, Detroit, London, Chicago, Johannesburg and Calcutta have failed to find in the city the anomic character posited by earlier sociologists.

Perhaps more significant for the Utopian view of the past is its romantic conception of history—a depiction of the small community of pre-industrial life as one at once kindlier, more spontaneous and humane than the world of today. That picture of a golden age of glorious Gemeinschaft ignores the tyranny of village hierarchies, the cruelty of a short lifespan and the deep constraints which close and constant surveillance imply. Accounts of personalism and humanization should also reckon with characterization of the social relationships of feudal society as ones which "extended and consolidated these methods by which men exploited men."[9] Not only was life capricious and at the mercy of disease, famine and banditry. The hierarchical relationships also gave those with power great capacities for cruelty, enrichment and liberty at the expense and impoverishment of those beneath them. The gap between the rich and the poor was often deep and impermeable; more akin to two orders of beings rather than a just relationship based on reciprocal duties and honored privileges. The "community" of man to man was by no means an unalloyed one but was also the community that excluded whole classes from its ties.

The mythic accounts of the past also often describe the present as more unlike the past than is warranted by scholarly analysis. In the community-society theory of social evolution, industrialization is held responsible for much of the present, as if the process of industrializing were all-powerful in changing other institutions. The dominance of the nuclear family in the modern society has thus been viewed as a response to the functional necessities of the modern economy. The small tight-knit nuclear group is viewed as better able to move from place to place according to market needs. But a more careful study of pre-industrial England indicates the existence and persistence of the nuclear family well before industry and suggests much incompatibility between modern production and the nuclear family. A number of studies of the current effect of industrialization in developing areas and in the history of Japan cast much doubt on the supposed disposition of pre-industrial social structures to impede or even to be affected by industrial development.

So too, in the debate over the virtue of the village and its threatened destruction by modernism, various forms of Gandhianism have contributed an idealized version of the little community. If it was stable in Indian history, it did not remain so whenever adequate opportunities arose for people to escape it. Today the difficulty of getting former villagers to return or to make the village even a temporary place of employment is very great in India.

In an answer to Gandhi, the Untouchable leader, B. R. Ambedkar, presented "the other side" of the case. In place of election to legislatures by individual votes, some Indian political delegates had suggested the 1947 constitution

H

make village councils (panchayats) the electoral unit. Dr. Ambedkar, in opposing this proposal said:

> The love of the intellectual Indian for the village community is, of course, infinite if not pathetic . . . I hold that these village republics have been the ruination of India . . . What is the village but a sink of localism, a den of ignorance, narrow-mindedness and communalism? I am glad that the Draft Constitution has discarded the village and adopted the individual as its unit.[10]

In the Indian context the debate is grounded in the existing villages and emerging urban societies. In the Western world the context of the little community is more historical. In both, however, the discussion is permeated by the speaker's attitude toward his present society and its social relations. Whatever the "truth" of the assertions about the past, the character of modern life, or the direction of social change, what is at stake is the attitude toward choices about the future.

Alienation: Modernity as Negative Reference

The concept of community again emerges as a contrast to the contemporary in theories which emphasize the consequences of technological rationalization for human relationships. Here modern society is seen as a social organization devoid of sources of affective loyalty. The key word to describe the situation is "alienation"—a sense of detachment and noninvolvement in experience, of remoteness from the sentiments of group membership, of estrangement from roles carried out in organizational life.

The theory of alienation constitutes one aspect of a perspective toward contemporary social organization which is often labelled mass society theory. In the view of mass theorists, group association is in a long process of decline in modern life. Not only are primary associations such as the family, the neighborhood and the work group, less and less effective in organizing the life of the individual into cohesive social relationships; larger secondary organizations, such as classes, occupations and organizations (including schools and governments) are also decreasingly effective in commanding the loyalty and emotional affect by which they have formerly organized group life. If the family is seen as the model or metaphor for community and the stock market that of society, the mass is to be illustrated by the television audience. It has no interaction with the performers. Audience members neither communicate with nor are influenced by the responses of other members. The group characteristics of class, ethnicity, sex, occupation are all irrelevant to the understanding of the mass. Within the large-scale organizational life of the modern world, human beings interact with little affect or influence over each other; what is left of the social bond is thin and close to the breaking point.

... Such a structure may be shown to be one in which intermediate relations of community, occupation and association are more or less inoperative, and therefore one in which the individual and primary group are directly related to the state and to nation-wide organizations. The members of mass society, then, are interconnected only by virtue of their common ties to national centers of communication and organization. It is in this sense that we speak of mass society as the *atomized* society.[11]

What distinguishes mass society theory from the critique of contemporary life embodied in the views of the "little community" proponents is its focus on the bureaucratic and organizational aspects of modern life rather than the urban or territorial. Bigness is only a possible condition of the qualities which create masses. It is the remoteness and lack of direct and human (i.e. self-conscious) interaction which constitutes for the mass theorist the quality of modern society inherent in its large, centralized organizations. The State, the school, the factory and even the activity of shopping are permeated by mass relations and marked by persons acting toward each other as categories rather than as individuals or even group members. The disappearance of communal relations is to be found, in this perspective, in rural as well as in urban contexts, Suburbia, though its residents may live in small settlements and in close proximity, is perhaps the most typical milieu for in it there exist families geared to the organizational and occupational contexts and demands of bureaucratic life.

What the two perspectives have in common, however, is their view of history; an age of communal and personal commitments has given way to a new era of human existence in which men lead atomistic, alienated social lives. Robert Nisbet, in a chapter fittingly entitled, "The Loss of Community," typifies this view:

> ... in the process of modern industrial and political development, established social contexts have become weak, and fewer individuals have the secure interpersonal relations which formerly gave meaning and stability to existence.[12]

By no means all streams of thought concerned with alienation and/or mass theory share this assumption of a "lost paradise" or see "societal" organization as unable to affect a viable human existence. The Marxist critique, for example, finds the alienating elements of modern life in its specific economic structure and not in technology or systems of rational organization *per se*. In this perspective "community" emerges as a future state attainable through a more rational and egalitarian use of technology and science. The past, as I have discussed in an earlier chapter, is not a "golden age" of community but the future can be. Socialism as an ideal emerges as a form of Gesellschaft through which mankind will pass in transition to Communism, the ultimate Gemeinschaft.

Communitarian Utopias: Community as the Future

The concept "Community" has had an even more direct relation to Utopian movements than that of its implicit use in the criticism of modern society. In the narrower sense, "utopian communities" and the "communitarian movement" have presented a specific vision of life based on the communal ideal. The appearance of such movements during the nineteenth and twentieth centuries in Europe, the United States and Japan is evidence of the depth and continuousness of the communal image in inspiring efforts to direct and generate social and cultural change.

In these contexts, the use of "community" as a source for the establishment of actual communities is no accident. The current use of "commune" to denote the most dramatic and frequent form of contemporary Utopian settlements points to the import of the "community-society" typology as a very real and vibrant motif in language and action.

We should not confuse the effort to establish communities with the effort to establish "community." The former is found when men and women withdraw from their societies and begin new settlements, from whatever motivation and to achieve whatever objectives. The latter, the establishment of community, is an attempt to build a social organization which will satisfy the desire for relations of communion, for a form of human relationship which, in its communal character, is contrasted with the nature of human relationships in the parent society which they have left. The former, the establishment of communities, is part of the history of utopian settlements, but the latter, the establishment of community, is the working of community as a Utopian ideal.

The concept of communitarianism has covered a variety of movements and utopian settlements, from the sectarian colonies of religious groups such as the Shakerites, to the Socialist-Zionist Kibbutzim, the ethical spirit of Brook Farm and the current counter-culture movement toward rural communes. In understanding the usage of "community" we distinguish between *experimental* and *communal* utopias. The reference is to the nineteenth- and twentieth-century efforts to develop new settlements following criteria of social organization which differed radically from those of the dominant society in which they existed.

Most of the utopian communities established in the United States during the nineteenth century were experimental rather than communal. While they were characteristically small and local arrangements, in which everyone gained familiarity with each other, the development of communal, Gemeinschaftliche relationships was seldom a major goal of the Utopian impulse. Responses to religious exclusion, to the striving for new political arrangements or for economic structures superior to the present, they appeared rather as strategic withdrawals from a resistant and repressing society or as demonstrations of what a new society could be like. As vehicles for change, they represented alternatives to revolution, as Marx and Engels quite accurately perceived Owenite and Fourier Utopian Socialism to be. As strategies for change, they sought to achieve a demonstration effect to show on a small scale what could be possible for the whole society. The idea of experimentation in social organization permeated the communitarian view and they could be described as conceiving of the community "as an insulated laboratory for testing social measures."[13]

In this perspective, "community" assumes a neutral character; a convenient and expeditious way to organize a social experiment or to live as a cult in a hostile society. The use of *communal relations* as an object of utopian settlements is more characteristic of the contemporary utopian movements, such as the commune of the 1960s, the various rural communities established in the wake of the anti-urban activity of the 1920s and 1930s and even the utopian settlements of Japan and the return to the village motifs of the neo-Gandhians in India.

For this view of utopian communitarianism, the Gesellschaft character of the modern is reprehensible and the small, natural commune is its contrast. Often the evolutionary scheme of late nineteenth-century European sociology is re-echoed in diatribes against modernism and the glorification of the past as providing "islands of collective security in the anomic sea of industrial civilization."[14] The restorationist myth of reviving a "lost paradise" has a prominent place in these settlements. An earlier historical period contrasts with great favor to the present: "It wasn't long ago that you [America] were all forests and free animals . . . But you, little America, have become modern and responsible . . .".[15]

The word "commune" has again come into common usage. Its connotations appear in the context of the critique of modernism and rationalized politics and economy. The with-drawal of men and women from the ambitions, institutions and concerns of the complex, industrial and scientific culture into simpler and small social organization is seen as a route to a less anxious, troubled and tyrannized life. The security and warmth of the total group is extolled and the new com-munity built along the lines of the extended family and the "traditional" village. Indeed, as Rosabeth Kanter has put it in her study of nineteenth- and twentieth-century American communes:

> . . . the grand Utopian visions of the past have been re-placed by a concern with relations in a small group. Instead of conceptions of alternative societies, what is emerging are conceptions of alternative families.[16]

Romanticism and Rationalization: The Perpetual Dialogue

The American communal movement of the 1960s is self-consciously a rejection of a society and a culture seen as too organized, too calculating and too much devoted to con-sumption, ambition and egotistic struggle. The "loss of community" is thus the replacement of simpler, more direct and satisfying human relationships by those which prize efficient production, the increase in material wealth and power. The debate over the value of industrial organization and the rationalization of life which has resulted is by no means a new one. The concept of community, as a contrast to contemporary industrialized forms, has much continuity to the critical resistance and opposition which emerged in the wake of nineteenth-century industrialization in Europe. A revulsion against rational thought and organization, technical and scientific growth and the secularization of spiritual life is a corollary of the centralizing and organizing character of life in industrial societies in Europe, in Japan and in the United States.

The Romantic sensibility was a major expression of this resistance and criticism. It appears in such diverse forms as the youth movements of early twentieth-century Europe, the romantic expression in music, monarchical and anti-democratic politics, and the nostalgic recreation of the past as an era of lost greatness. What gives unity to such seemingly diverse activities is the extolling of sentiment and feeling as superior to but corrupted by reason, science and technical organization. In this use of "community" there is a tendency to find in the simple, traditional folk-like society the elements of moral virtues which contrast with modern life. In his study of the French men of letters in the nineteenth century. César Graña remarks:

> Creatures of urban civilization that they were, the literary rebels often suspected cosmopolitanism and yearned after remote and unspoiled societies. The uniqueness of national and regional life became a stylistic and psychological passion. So did the hatred of technology, the violator of nature's mystery and integrity, and the love of craftsmanship—a personal, intimate, subjective mode of production.[17]

In its scorn for the bourgeoisie—supporters of a rational and utilitarian view of life and society—and in its resentment of the subversion of the traditional authority of cultural elites, the Romantic movement has many of the aspects of an aristocratic critique of modern life. The glorification of the hero, the Superman and the man of unique genius apart from the herd, provided further evidence that modern life crushes individuality in the maws of a technical, mass-like machine.

Community as Millennial Utopia

There is more to the utopian strain of communitarianism than the restorationist motif. Used as a contrast to the isolation, the routine and the constraints of *Gesellschaft* and Society it is also imbued with the ideals of a new and distinct mode of life; one in which the evils of the present are resolved and the evils of the past avoided.

Within the current commune movement, for example, the motif of community as family is accompanied by the often contradictory theme of community as the arena of the spontaneous and the "free." Here the tenets are expressed in the language of "personal growth" or "self-actualization" in contrast to a society in which people use each other as instruments to calculated ends. "Doing your own thing" is a persistent morality and limits the contrasting spirit of communal involvement as well as opposing the ethics of routinization.

It is this seemingly inconsistent melding of individuation and personal relationships, a union of the "inner-directed" and the "other-directed", that has been a persistent theme in the ideals of many movements. It has also played an important part in the humanistic Socialism which has so often guided modern political utopias.

While Marx and Engels excoriated the nonscientific, Utopian theme beloved of Socialists of the communitarian phase, the impulse remains a significant one. The emphasis on the development of fellow-feeling, of a cooperative rather than a competitive spirit, and of equality of dignity and status has shown the significance of the small community as a basic source for a reconstruction of man, which is taken to be the most important task of social reconstruction. Thus in his critique of revolutionary socialism of the Marxist variety, Martin Buber has argued that a humane and nonauthoritarian Socialism must emerge out of utopian development: "it must be built up of little societies on the basis of communal life and of the associations of these societies."[18]

Here again we have the usage of community in contrast to society. Buber insists that the Utopian ideal of Marx and Lenin is only another version of the Gesellschaft—another form of coercive politics and bureaucratized economic organization.

> The most valuable of all goods—the life between man and man—gets lost in the process; the autonomous relationships become meaningless, personal relationships wither; and the very spirit of man hires itself out as a functionary.[19]

Buber's vision of a society of decentralized Gemeinschaftliche communities built around common production has much in common with Durkheim's view of professional associations. And so we have come full circle. The problem of the sociologists of the late nineteenth century has been transmuted in an era of declining aristocracies and incipient industrialization to a period of egalitarian democracies and bureaucratized organization.

The Communal Ideal

If we perceive the debate over the question of community-society not as a scientific discussion of analytic theories but of the quality of contemporary life, our understanding of the terms is placed in a different context. It is not pertinent to ask if the past has *really* approximated the "community" or if the march of change leads straight on to "society." Rather, it is relevant to examine the present and to adopt an attitude toward it.

Critics of Marxian and other writers who see modern life

as alienating the individual from work, family, neighborhood and politics are quick to point out that dubious assumptions of human nature underlie such assertions. The experience of alienation, of remoteness and noncommitment describes a subjective attitude of persons. Since the human being today is not necessarily the same as the human being of the past, his experiences, including a view of the past, depend upon his expectations. What might have been acceptable, even preferred, in Victorian England may be anathema to the resident of London in the 1970s. Even to expect the demand that work be interesting, marriages be happy and political participation be constant is itself the mark of a new historical period. One cannot use the criteria of one age to evaluate another. Bernard Shaw expressed this wittily when he said: "Do not do unto others what you would have them do unto you. Their tastes may be different."

The theorist propounding the alienation of what is modern may drop the demand for a subjective experience of alienation. He may insist that the position of many in the modern world is that of an alienation from a possible, or "truer" nature. To do this, however, requires some assumption of a common kind of human nature, equally discoverable in the past and the present but much more realizable in that past. This creates great philosophical difficulties for any view of human beings which stresses their choice as an element in governing their values.

Yet it is immaterial whether or not the past approached the characteristics of the communal ideal. We might even find, as a scientific proposition, that the present is more communal than the past. This has little bearing on the demands that we may make for change in the direction of communal relations. We live within the experience of our lives and measure them, not against the past, but against what we conceive to be possible and to be needed. Each age is the judge of its own utopias.

Put this way the ideology of community and the utopian movements of communitarianism are expressions of the concern of modern men with the specific quality of life today.

Whatever the theory of social change or the view of history they espouse, some would emphasize the constraining, limiting rigidity of organization; some the impersonal, categorizing and rationalistic manner of bureaucracy and economic relationships. Most see the family as the model of what is lacking in modern life. The taken for granted trust and loyalty of kinship does not depend on the productive performance of the child or the parent. The ability to express emotion grants the spontaneity of behavior for which many critics of modern life yearn. The anonymous and often anxious relations between strangers of the large cities of our times seems absent in the small communities of the mind upon which utopian settlements and communes are founded.

Above all, the communal ideal emphasizes the attachments between men (in the general sense) based on what they possess in common: their human capacity to hurt and to be hurt; to love and to be loved; to shame and to feel shame; to be cruel and to abhor cruelty. Communitarian movements so often contrast the ethical character of small local communities with that of the urban and organizational quality of the total society. It is not recognition of a necessarily correct relation between size and the quality of life. Rather, it is an anguished cry against those facets of modern life in which men and women are categorized, isolated, typed and in which their specific qualities as human beings and as emotive and dependent persons is ignored.

That much of this is expressed in the language of social science is no peculiar accident. Science is the idiom of our age and we operate with the need to ground our moral decisions in factual necessities. The scientific, semantic meanings of sociology are not sufficient to grant significance and moral direction on their own. They do enable the student to isolate the issues. But the infusion of dramatic, poetic, distorting meaning is essential to give the scientific concepts vitality and significance for relevant human concerns. That the concept of Community has had so constant a usage is testimony both to its power and to the ubiquitousness of its ideal.

Notes to Chapter 4

[1] Peter Winch, *The Idea of a Social Science*, New York and London, 1958; p. 123.

[2] Kenneth Burke, *The Philosophy of Literary Form*, New York; p. 142.

[3] Fritz Pappenheim, *The Alienation of Modern Man*, New York, 1959; p. 81.

[4] Richard Hofstadter, *The Age of Reform*, New York, 1955; pp. 23–36.

[5] Arthur Vidich and Joseph Bensman, *Small Town in Mass Society*, Princeton, N.J., 1958; p. 33.

[6] Harvey Zorbaugh, *The Gold Coast and the Slum*, Chicago, 1929; p. 80.

[7] Robert Park, "The City as a Social Laboratory" (orig. pub. 1929) in Ralph H. Turner, ed., *Robert E. Park on Social Control and Collective Behavior*, Chicago, 1967; p. 18.

[8] Louis Wirth, "The Scope and Problems of the Community" (orig. pub. 1933) in Albert J. Reiss, Jr., *Louis Wirth on Cities and Social Life*, Chicago, 1964; p. 168.

[9] Marc Bloch, *Feudal Society*, Chicago: Phoenix Books, 1963; p. 443.

[10] Constituent Assembly Debates, Vol. VII, p. 39. Quoted in Hugh Tinker "Tradition and Experiment in Forms of Government" in C. H. Philips, ed., *Politics and Society in India*, London, 1963; pp. 155–86.

[11] William Kornhauser, *The Politics of Mass Society*, Glencoe, Illinois, 1959; pp. 74–5.

[12] Robert Nisbet, *Community and Power* (orig. pub. 1953), New York and London, 1962; p. 15.

[13] Arthur Bestor, *Backwoods Utopias*, Philadelphia, 1950; p. 18.

[14] Yoshi Sugihara and David Plath, *Sensei and his People* Berkeley and Los Angeles: University of California Press, 1969; p. 187.

[15] S. Darlington, *San Francisco Express Times*.

[16] Quoted in Michael Goodman, *The Movement Towards a New America*, New York, 1970; p. 33.

[17] Rosabeth Kanter, *Commitment and Community*, Cambridge, Mass., 1972; p. 165.

[18] César; Graña, *Modernity and its Discontents*, New York, 1967; p. 65.

[19] Martin Buber, *Paths in Utopia* (orig. pub. 1969), Boston, 1958; p. 81.

[20] Ibid., p. 132.

BIBLIOGRAPHY

This section will indicate some of the major sources of materials developed in the essay. I have also added some additional sources which are useful for the student who wishes to go further into ideas or materials suggested by this book. It is not meant as an exhaustive bibliography on the subject but only as a starter for those whose interest goes beyond the limits of this work.

1. General Works

The most useful general analysis of the community concept in nineteenth-century thought is found in Robert Nisbet's *Social Change and History* (Oxford University Press, 1969). A short discussion with much reference to earlier historical antecedents is in a lecture by Donald G. Macrae, "Ages and Stages" (August Comte Memorial Trust Lecture No. 9, University of London: The Athlone Press, 1973).

2. Émile Durkheim

There is an enormous amount of literature on Durkheim. The discussion of mechanical and organic solidarity is embedded in general analyses of Durkheim's work. The major work is still Talcott Parsons, *The Structure of Social Action* (McGraw-Hill Book Co., 1937). A valuable study of Durkheim's social context in nineteenth-century politics is found in H. Stuart Hughes, *Consciousness and Society* (Vintage Books, 1958). Recently there has been a spate of work on Durkheim. I have found the following most useful for this work: Gianfranco Poggi, *Images of Society* (Stanford University Press, 1972); Steven Lukes, *Emile Durkheim* (Allen Lane, 1973), especially Chapters 7–9; Ernest Wallwork, *Durkheim: Morality and Milieu* (Harvard University Press, 1972), especially Chapter 4. For a critical appraisal of Durkheimian principles, see Jack D. Douglas, *The Social Meanings of Suicide* (Princeton University Press, 1967).

3. *Modernization Theory*

The works of Robert Redfield have been of significance in developing a scheme of evolutionary stages and a set of contrasts between folk and urban settlements. See *The Folk Culture of Yucatan* (University of Chicago Press, 1941) and "The Folk Society" (*American Journal of Sociology*, 52, 1947, pp. 293–308). His later works on peasant societies and on "the little community" are also highly influential. See *Peasant Society and Culture* (University of Chicago Press, 1956) and *The Little Community* (University of Chicago Press, 1955). Another influential scheme of contrasts has been that of Howard Becker, "Current Sacred-Secular Theory and its Development," in Howard Becker and Alvin Boskoff, ed., *Modern Sociological Theory* (Holt, Rinehart and Winston, Inc., 1957).

The major thrust toward sociological analysis of the so-called "underdeveloped" countries and the problem of industrial growth is found among exponents of modernization theory. This can be found, in varying forms of expression, in the following works: Gabriel Almond, "A Functional Approach to Comparative Politics" in Gabriel Almond and James Coleman, *The Politics of Developing Areas* (Princeton

University Press, 1960); S. N. Eisenstadt, *Modernization: Protest and Change* (Prentice-Hall, 1966); Bert Hoselitz, *Sociological Sources of Economic Growth* (Free Press, 1960); "Development and the Theory of Social Systems" in Manfred Stanley, ed., *Social Development*, Chapter 2 (Basic Books, 1972); Bert Hoselitz and Wilbert Moore, ed., *Industrialization and Society* (UNESCO-Mouton, 1963), especially papers by Hoselitz, Moore and Neil Smelser; Clark Kerr, John Dunlop, Fred Harbison and Charles Myers, *Industrialism and Industrial Man* (Harvard University Press, 1960); Joseph Kahl, *The Measurement of Modernism* (The University of Texas Press, 1968); Daniel Lerner and Lucille Pevsner, *The Passing of Traditional Society* (The Free Press, 1958); Wilbert Moore, *Social Change* (Prentice-Hall, 1963).

Modernization theory has been critically analyzed along the lines of interest of this essay in Reinhard Bendix, "Tradition and Modernity Reconsidered," *Comparative Studies in Society and History*, IX, (1966–7), pp. 292–346; Joseph Gusfield, "Tradition and Modernity: Misplaced Polarities in the Study of Social Change," *American Journal of Sociology*, 72 (January, 1967), pp. 351–62 and "The Social Construction of Tradition" in John Legge, ed., *Traditional Styles and Political Leadership* (Melbourne University Press, 1973), pp. 83–104.

4. *Sources of Communal Identity*

Tomatsu Shibutani and Kian Kwan, *Ethnic Stratification* (Macmillan, 1965) is a superb mine of insights and information on the general problem of communal identity. Clifford Geertz, ed. *Old Societies and New States* (The Free Press, 1963) is an excellent collection of papers on issues of communalism in new nations. Especially note the papers by Geertz, Marriott and Shils. Reinhard Bendix, *Nation-Building and Citizenship* is a fine analysis of the problem of integration of groups into a political community in both Western European and British historical experience and

I

in that of non-Western countries, especially India and Japan.

Much of the analysis of ethnicity in this essay has utilized American sources, with the exception of Everett C. Hughes' classic study, *French-Canada in Transition* (University of Chicago Press, 1943). Also see his general work *When Peoples Meet: Racial and Ethnic Frontiers* (The Free Press, 1952). Among studies of ethnicity in America the work by Nathan Glazer and Daniel Moynihan, *Beyond the Melting Pot* (The M.I.T. Press, 1971) is especially vivid and detailed. Milton Gordon, *Assimilation in American Life* (Oxford University Press, 1964) is a good general account. Recent statements relating to the ethnic conflict revival in the United States are found in Andrew Greeley, *Why Can't They Be Like Us?* (E. P. Dutton, 1971); Michael Novak, *The Rise of the Unmeltable Ethnics* (Macmillan, 1972) and Richard Scammon and Ben Wattenberg, *The Real Majority* (Coward-McAnn, 1970). Edward Laumann, "The Social Structure of Religious and Ethno-religious Groups in a Metropolitan Community," *American Sociological Review*, 34 (April, 1969) pp. 182–97, is among the best of recent sociological studies. The study of the Hawaiian Chinese cited in the text is in Clarence Glick, "The Relation Between Position and Status in the Assimilation of the Chinese in Hawaii," *American Journal of Sociology*, 47 (March, 1942) pp. 667–79. For a study of ethnic and religious conflict in American history see Joseph Gusfield, *Symbolic Crusade* (University of Illinois Press, 1963). The materials related to the social construction of tradition are explored in greater detail in my "Social Construction of Tradition," op. cit. above. For the materials on the tradition of the Japanese emperor see Herschel Webb, "The Development of an Orthodox Attitude toward the Imperial Institution in the Nineteenth Century," in Marius Jensen, ed., *Changing Japanese Attitudes Toward Modernization* (Princeton University Press, 1965) pp. 167–92. Analyses of language movements in India are discussed in detail in Jyotirindra Das Gupta, *Language, Conflict and National Development* (University of California Press, 1970). The shifting conceptions of black culture are discussed in papers by Robert Blauner and by Roy Bryce-Laporte in Norman Whitten, Jr. and John Swed, ed., *Anglo-American Anthropology* (The Free Press, 1970).

The conception of community as common territory has a vast literature. The student can find an entree into this perspective through the following: Roland Warren, *The Community in America* (Rand, MacNally and Co., 1963); Leo Schnore, "The Community," in Neil Smelser, ed., *Sociology* (John Wiley and Sons, 1973) and Robert M. French, ed., *The Community: A Comparative Perspective* (F. E. Peacock, Inc., 1969). A classic discussion is Robert McIver, *Community* (London: Macmillan, 1924).

5. *Levels of Integration and Arenas of Communal Action*

A basic general discussion of areas of communal behavior is in Julian Steward, *Area Research: Theory and Practice* (Social Science Research Council Bulletin, 63, 1950). The now classic paper, referred to in the text, is J. B. Barnes, "Class and Committees in a Norwegian Island Parish," *Human Organization,* VII (February, 1954). (Reprinted in R. French, op. cit. above.) Elizabeth Bott, *Family and Social Network* (Tavistock Publications, 1957) is another excellent usage of a somewhat similar idea applied to the concept of class. Arthur Vidich and Joseph Bensman, *Small Town in Mass Society* is a superb analysis of the impact between different levels of the same society.

The distinctions between different countries and cultures in fixing boundaries of group membership is especially pertinent in Chie Nakane's comparison of India and Japan in *Japanese Society* (University of California Press, 1970). On India, see M. N. Srinivas, *Social Change in Modern India* (University of California Press, 1966). The function of caste associations and ethnic groups in urban migration is examined, for India, in N. K. Bose, "Calcutta: A Premature Metropolis," *Scientific American,* 213 (September, 1965), pp. 90–102 and for West Africa in Kenneth Little, *West African Urbanization* (Cambridge University Press, 1965).

6. *Stratification and Segmentation*

For a collection of important papers on comparative social stratification, the student is recommended to S. M. Lipset and Reinhard Bendix, ed., *Class, Status and Power* (second ed., The Free Press, 1966). The idea of "closed and open" forms of stratification is especially well treated, in general and in the Indian context, by F. G. Bailey and also by André Beteille in papers in *The European Journal of Sociology*, 7 (1966). The latter paper is also reprinted in a valuable set of papers on Indian castes in André Beteille, *Castes: Old and New* (Asia Publishing House, 1969).

The system of stratification and segmentation in relation to Indian caste systems is amply discussed in several major works among Indian studies. In addition to Beteille's above, the following are significant: M. N. Srinivas, *Caste in Modern India* (Asia Publishing House, 1962); David Mandelbaum, *Society in India*, Vols. I and II (University of California Press, 1970); and M. Singer and B. S. Cohn, ed., *Structure and Change in Indian Society* (Viking Fund Publications in Anthropology, No. 47, 1968), especially papers by Srinivas and by Rowe. Several important studies are André Beteille, *Caste, Class and Power* (University of California Press, 1965), Robert Hardgrave, *The Nadars of Tamilnad* (University of California Press, 1969); Owen Lynch, *The Politics of Untouchability* (Columbia University Press, 1969); and Lloyd and Susanne Rudolph, *The Modernity of Tradition* (University of Chicago Press, 1967). For a significant but very different approach to caste, see Louis Dumont, *Homo Hierarchicus* (University of Chicago Press, 1970). An excellent study of American ethnic groups in the economy is by Ivan Light, *Ethnic Enterprise in America* (University of California Press, 1972).

In developing the concept of social segmentation I have

derived much from the discussion of Marx, stratification and politics in Ralf Dahrendorf, *Class and Class Conflict in Industrial Society* (Stanford University Press, 1959). Some of these ideas were utilized in the context of Indian education in Joseph Gusfield, "Education and Social Segmentation in Modern India," in Joseph Fischer, ed., *The Social Sciences and the Comparative Study of Educational Systems* (International Textbook Company, 1970).

Much of the material in this section bears on the issues of national development. The two previously cited works, *Old Societies and New States*, edited by Clifford Geertz and *Nation Building and Citizenship* by Reinhard Bendix are especially pertinent.

7. *Community as Utopia*

Several books analyzing "the decline of community" in the modern world state the general theme under consideration here. Of these Robert Nisbet, *Community and Power* (Galaxy Books, 1962) and Maurice Stein, *The Eclipse of Community* (Princeton University Press, 1960) are valuable statements. The analysis of urbanism is best represented by the Chicago school of sociology during the 1920s to the 1940s. For the leading statements of that discussion, see Robert Park, *The City* (University of Chicago Press, 1925) and the collections of papers in Ralph Turner, ed., *Robert E. Park on Social Control and Collective Behavior* (Phoenix Books, 1967) and Albert J. Reiss, Jr., ed., *Louis Wirth on Cities and Social Behavior* (Phoenix Books, 1964).

The concept of alienation in the context of the community discussion has a number of statements. The best, inclusive and detailed analysis of the alienation concept is in Joachim Israels, *Alienation: From Marx to Modern Sociology* (Allyn and Bacon, 1971). Also see the influential paper by Melvin Seeman, "On the Meaning of Alienation," *American Sociological Review*, XXVI (1961), 753–8; William Kornhauser, *The Politics of Mass Society* (The Free Press, 1959); Fritz

Pappenheim, *The Alienation of Modern Man* (Monthly Review Press, 1959); and César Graña, *Modernity and its Discontents* (Harper Torchbooks, 1967).

Many aspects of nineteenth- and twentieth-century communitarianism have been discussed in my *Utopian Myths and Movements in Modern Societies* (General Learning Press Module, 1973). For nineteenth-century American communitarianism, the leading work is Arthur Bestor, *Backwoods Utopias* (University of Pennsylvania Press, 1950). On British utopian communities, see W. H. G. Armytage, *Heavens Below* (University of Toronto Press, 1961). On contemporary American communes see Rosabeth Kanter, *Commitment and Community* (Harvard University Press, 1972). A major statement of the communal ideal as a utopian force is that by Martin Buber, *Paths in Utopia* (Beacon Press, 1958). An important but overlooked paper on the place of the communal ideal in socialist and communist thought is that of Stanley Moore, "Utopian Themes in Marx and Mao," *Monthly Review*, June, 1969.

8. *Conceptualization, Typologies and Concept Formation*

The issues of concepts and types discussed in this essay are still best elucidated in Max Weber, *Methodology of the Social Sciences* (translated and edited by Edward Shils and Henry A. Finch, The Free Press, 1949). It is a difficult book and students might also begin with the various positions represented by papers in *Philosophy of the Social Sciences*, edited by Maurice Natanson (Random House, 1963), especially papers by Hempel and Schutz. Another useful work for discussion of these issues is Peter Winch, *The Idea of a Social Science* (Routledge and Kegan Paul, Ltd., 1958).

The general perspective toward the meaning and reality of concepts utilized in this essay can be found in several works of the symbolic interactionist and phenomenological "schools" in sociology. Among these see Herbert Blumer, *Symbolic Interactionism*, especially Chapter 1 (Prentice-Hall,

1969); Peter Berger and Thomas Luckmann, *The Social Construction of Reality* (Doubleday and Co., 1966); Barney Glaser and Anselm Strauss, *The Discovery of Grounded Theory* (Aldine, 1967); and Alfred Schutz, "Concept and Theory Formation in the Social Sciences," in Dorothy Emmett and Alasdair MacIntyre, ed., *Sociological Theory and Philosophical Analysis* (Macmillan, 1970). The perspective toward concepts as dualisms owes much to a significant paper by Reinhard Bendix and Bennett Berger, "Images of Society and Problems of Concept Formation in Sociology," in Llewellyn Gross, ed., *Symposium on Sociological Theory* (Row, Peterson and Co., 1959).

The above are all pertinent to issues of ideal-types in sociological method. Especially useful, in addition, is the paper by John McKinney, "Sociological Theory and the Process of Typification," in John McKinney and Edward Tiryakian, ed., *Theoretical Sociology* (Appleton-Century-Crofts, 1970), pp. 235–70; Stanford Lyman and Marvin Scott, "Accounts," in their *Sociology of the Absurd* (Appleton-Century-Crofts, 1970); and especially Alfred Schutz, *The Phenomenology of the Social World*, translated by F. Lehnert and M. Walsh (Northwestern University Press, 1967), especially Part 1.

Concepts as metaphors or myths is a major theme of much literary analysis. The most brilliant and indispensable analysis is by Kenneth Burke. In *A Rhetoric of Motives* and *A Grammar of Motives* he has outlined a seminal approach to language and concept formation. I have also made use of his essay "Semantic and Poetic Meanings" in *The Philosophy of Literary Forms* (Louisiana State University Press, 1967). Two other useful discussions of myth and metaphor in literary analysis are Northrop Frye, *The Anatomy of Criticism* (Princeton University Press, 1957) and Phillip Wheelwright, *Metaphor and Reality* (Indiana University Press, 1964). An important analysis by a philosopher is Max Black, *Models and Metaphors* (Cornell University Press, 1962) especially Chapter 3 and Chapter 13.

INDEX

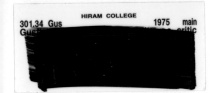